ART NOUVEAU

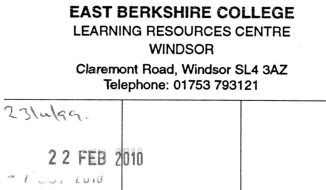

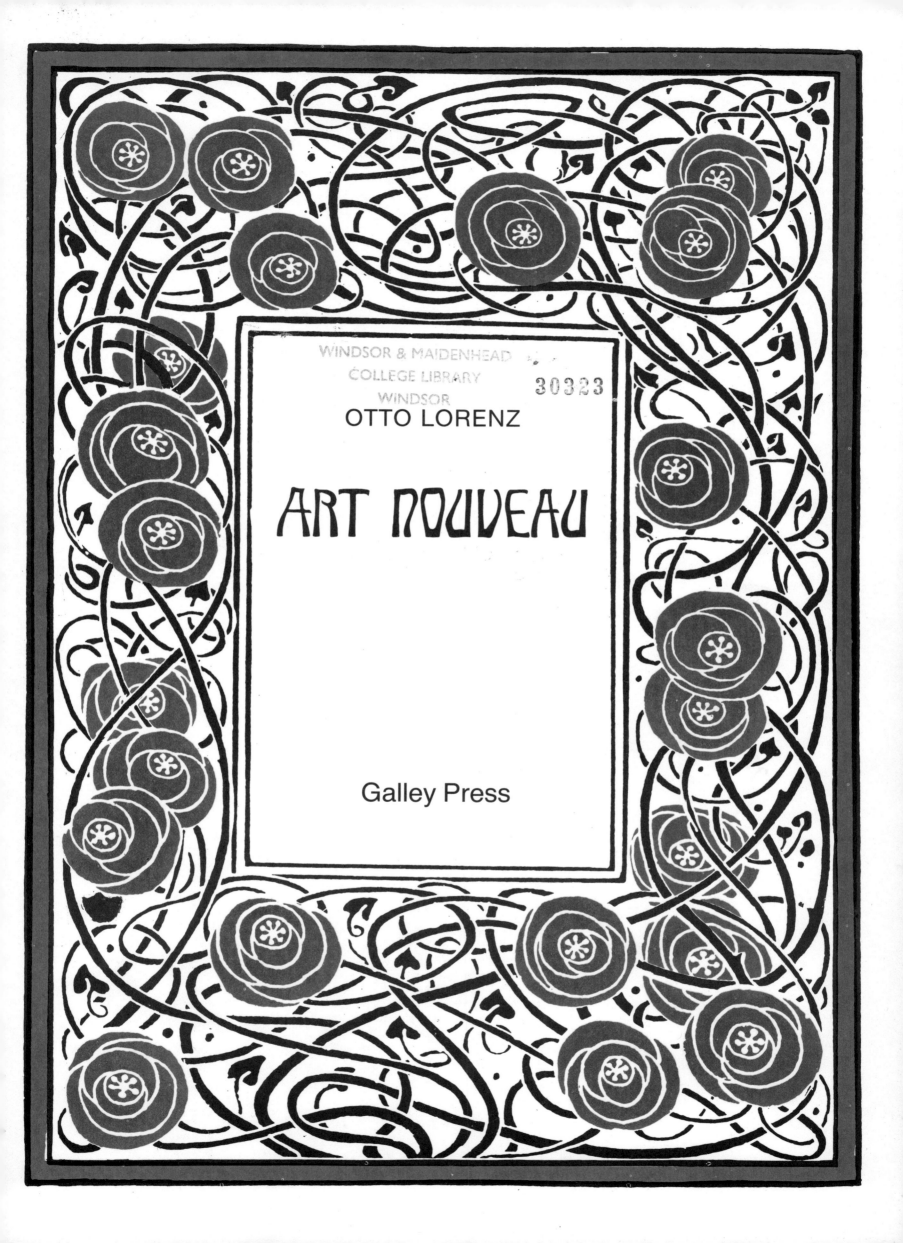

OTTO LORENZ

ART NOUVEAU

Galley Press

709.44Ł OR

Introduction

Art Nouveau is an artistic renewal movement which began in the middle of the 19th Century and is still having an influence on all styles and areas of art.

The nomenclature varied as much as the characteristics of individual works. In England it was at first spoken of as "Modern Style". In France it was "Style Moderne" in order to express the derivation of the new art from English cultural circles. In Holland they called the trend "Nieuwe Kunst" before the term "Art Nouveau" prevailed everywhere except in Germany. This term derives from the name of an art gallery set up in Paris in 1895 by Samuel Bing of Hamburg, near the legendary Passage de L'Opera. The opening of the gallery was advertised by a particularly effective poster in the new style by Felix Vallotton. The name that came to be used in Germany, "Jugendstil", is taken from the title of a journal Jugend (Youth) which devoted itself to this style.

The term Art Nouveau was at first only used in the area of applied art and crafts. In painting it has only been used with historical hindsight – and even then only hesitantly.

The characteristic elements of Art Nouveau are: the stress on the ornamental, the heavy stylisation by rhythmic overemphasis on form and the dominance of line. Frequently in this context the relation between Art Nouveau and Gothic art is referred to. Indeed there is a whole series of parallels, as much in the basic ideas on which both styles are founded as in the decorative aspects. Of course it should not be forgotten that the artists of the late 19th and early 20th centuries were no strangers to the historical and cultural devices of Gothic art.

The most important decoration in the new art was the creeping plant motif. Figures express the style of the time in their elongated feminine forms, dressed in long flowing robes; dancers and walkers are frozen in mid-step, with animals of extreme elegance like swans or cranes. The representation of realistic workers, which was a natural concern to the expressionist painters, was unknown to Art Nouveau. At best, the persons portrayed are involved in some kind of activity, yet it is not the activity which is most important, but the appearance of the person doing it.

In arts and crafts as well as in architecture and interior design, the new trend went hand in hand with a consideration of the craftsman's skill. This was an especially fruitful symbiosis and the works it produced frequently combined an aesthetically pleasing novelty with completely appropriate use of materials. Well produced household articles had a high value in people's ordinary life well into the 20's. So expedience and fitness of materials were high on the list of criteria for the creators of Art Nouveau.

Art Nouveau was an attempt to create a generally binding canon of form which would be a new way of life, a search for inner meaning without the stylistic burden of the previous artistic development of external expression.

The new style was first and formost an expression of a new direction of the spirit. Sincerity was the basis of the new ideas. Just as *Jugend* described itself in its subtitle as "a weekly journal of culture and life", so every thought and wish of the artist was geared to the whole of life. The artists claimed to want to exert a reforming influence on every area of life and of the mind. The various plastic arts as well as literature, dance, theatre, and also architecture, illustration, interior design and the manufacture of consumer goods were all encompassed in a comprehensive overview.

Admittedly the roots of the downfall of the movement lay in this promise of a total effect. Its strengths were not sufficient for a comprehensive reform of life on all levels. What the movement's spiritual leaders were creating were things which in the end, because of their absolute quality, could only be produced for an élite minority. Only a small circle of people could afford books from Insel, glass from Gallé or furniture by Peter Behrens. The processes of industrial mass production grasped avidly at Art Nouveau ornamentation but their products, devoid of any real quality, had only the appearance of artistic skill. The ornamentation epidemic had begun. Within a few decades Art Nouveau had swamped daily life to such an extent that the public's willingness to take it all in was exhausted, especially as more and more pointless uses were found for it.

"You can't go out in the street any more without banging your head on an Art Nouveau candelabrum" one critic finally wrote. Reproductions by anonymous industrial manufacturers led things to absurdity and caused a drift into mere gaudy show.

In a satirical contribution to the German magazine *Jugend* (of which more later) by Gumppenberg, this trend was harshly condemned: "Jugend recently came before God in Heaven, wearing such a lo-o-ong face. The Lord received it cordially, asking how things were going, how many advertising contracts had it had, whether anyone had had it locked up yet, and finally, why it was so angry. 'Dear Lord God', said Jugend, 'They're ruining my good name! Or rather they're abusing it. People are making scandalous objects down there out of plaster, cardboard, leather, zinc, and what have you, and then, as it were, putting it on my bill. Art Nouveau they call it, when they've pressed out or stickered on or doubled over a cigarette case or cashbox or a photoframe that's half human and half ornamentation and as distorted as possible. Every sheet of wallpaper, every piece of calico is called Art Nouveau if the pattern is half horrible and half Japanese. Chairs you can't sit on, cupboards you can't put things in, glasses you can't drink out of, spoons you can't eat with are all called Art Nouveau. It's enough to drive you mad! I simply can't imagine that I invented this style. All I did was encourage it and cultivate certain strengths. And now it seems I have to bear the cost of all the misunderstandings and excrescences, for all the trans-mogrifications of a crude mass industry which only produces Art Nouveau because rococo designs are no longer in. These chaps overlook the fact that I've produced a great number of good and beautiful things for which I would happily take as mine the title of Art Nouveau. I don't like it anymore! I'm not going along with it any more. I'm getting out! I'm going to get myself rechristened!'"

In 1941 Fredrich Ahlers-Hestermann began his fundamental work *Stilwende* (turning point of style) which once again made the general public aware of the real basics of Art Nouveau, with the words: "The vision which the words Art Nouveau engenders in us is ridiculous and dreadful. Plant-like reptiles wind themselves around remodelled sofas, improbable masses of hair on concave women's heads make ashtrays and a few sea-roses have succeeded in estab-lishing themselves on coloured-tiled ovens." And in another place he writes further about the extent of Art Nouveau. "It was beautiful like an important play, the way the lines rolled on like a flood, the crashing onslaught of which demolished the rotten, the outmoded, and the dull things of existence. As it ebbed, liquid and sparkling, it left foul-smelling jellyfish and seaweed. Those are the remains we are still aware of. Few of us know that world, like the world of the crystal depths of the sea, to which they all belong: these misconceived, cheapened industrialised, distorted images of the skill and ideas of the artists."

Forty years later such shocking visions disappeared. Today's young people come upon Art Nouveau as a new discovery, and time has shown that the style influenced the future. The Art Nouveau movement became the great source of inspiration for the moderns. It is no coincidence that the roots of all the move-ments of intellectual progress which gave hope to the people of the 20th Cen-tury lie in the years of Art Nouveau.

"We are now seeing signs that there will be a new style," wrote Peter Behrens. "Not something arising out of the old one; that is to say it is partly already here, at least in its beginnings. Of course, we must keep our eyes open and have a joy-ful will and a belief in beauty. Then we will recognise that something is coming into being that corresponds more deeply to our lives than those artificially bizarre forms which outwardly appear modern but are mostly just some people's easy merchandising, a quick way of earning a living. That which is coming into being has an inner influence and is neither concocted at random nor playfully lumped together with the old."

The years of Art Nouveau were at the same time the beginning of what is described as Exhibition Art. The democratisation of the artistic trades had turned the artist into an economic factor. The traditional dependence of the artist on a patron from the ruling classes was rapidly disappearing. (It was more and more a case of the upper classes having to patronise the artist rather than the onus being on the artist himself). The dependence on the church as a source of commissions had earlier been broken. Art now had to find a market place.

Even successful artists whose talents were recognised or who had connections with official bodies, now had to distinguish themselves in terms of how well their exhibitions were received. All the others needed to create an audience in order to become known and therefore earn a living.

The creation of an audience happened on the one hand because of large, officially sponsored exhibitions, like the World Expositions at which plenty of space was given over to fine arts and crafts. But it also happened through the coming together of likeminded artists in groups who organised 'salons' and thereby created a mouthpiece to wider sections of the populace.

The various journals also made contributions, as did private initiative. Friends of art were buyers who at the same time helped the artists to step into the limelight in their own galleries.

"This exhibition art, as it was already being called in 1900, was also the result of the institutionalised dialogue between producers and consumers. These circumstances made exhibitions possible since, while they did not force people to buy, they did bring together many and varied individual pieces for potential sale. There was also the passionate relationship between 'exhibitionist' art and 'voyeur' viewers". (Simon).

(As well as the journals which specifically dealt with Art Nouveau such as *Pan, Jugend, Insel, Simplicissimus* and *Ver Sacrum*, which will be treated in the chapter on the importance of printed graphics, a large number of publications contained articles explaining Art Nouveau – admittedly occasionally from a negative point of view.)

Wider readerships were reached, particularly in questions of interior design and taste, by *Dekorative Kunst* (Decorative Art), *Deutsche Kunst und Dekoration* (German Art and Decoration) and *Die Kunst fur Alle* (Art for All). Politically orientated journals like *Die Zukunft* (The Future), *Die Zeit* (The Times), *Die Gegenwart* (The Present) or *Die Neue Rundschau* (New Review) seldom concerned themselves with the art themes. When they did however, their opinions tended to be biased. Finally there was a whole series of very widely distributed publications like *Der Kunstwart* (Artward!) which was read in conservatives circles and inclined towards populist or sometimes even naturalist art, and occasionally advertised Art Nouveau artists or their works for their own aims. Altogether, the periodicals had a considerable influence on the dissemination of the new art.

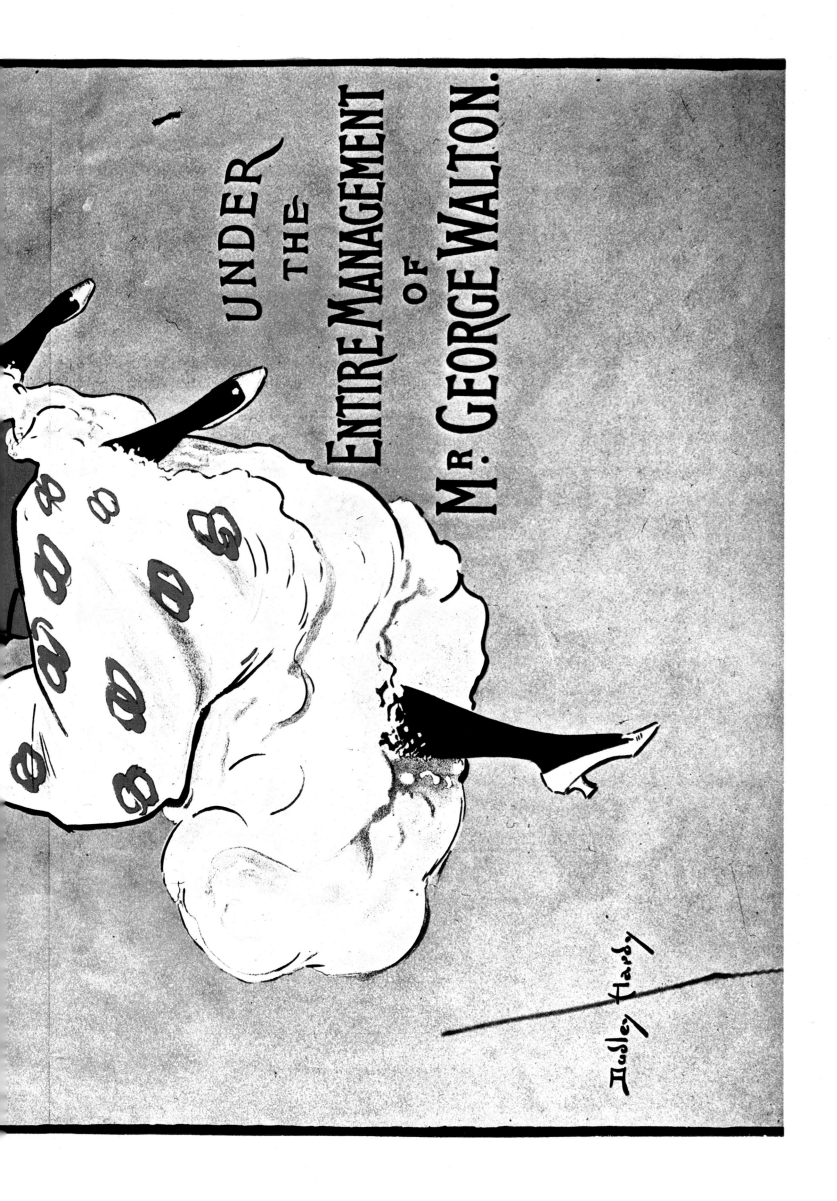

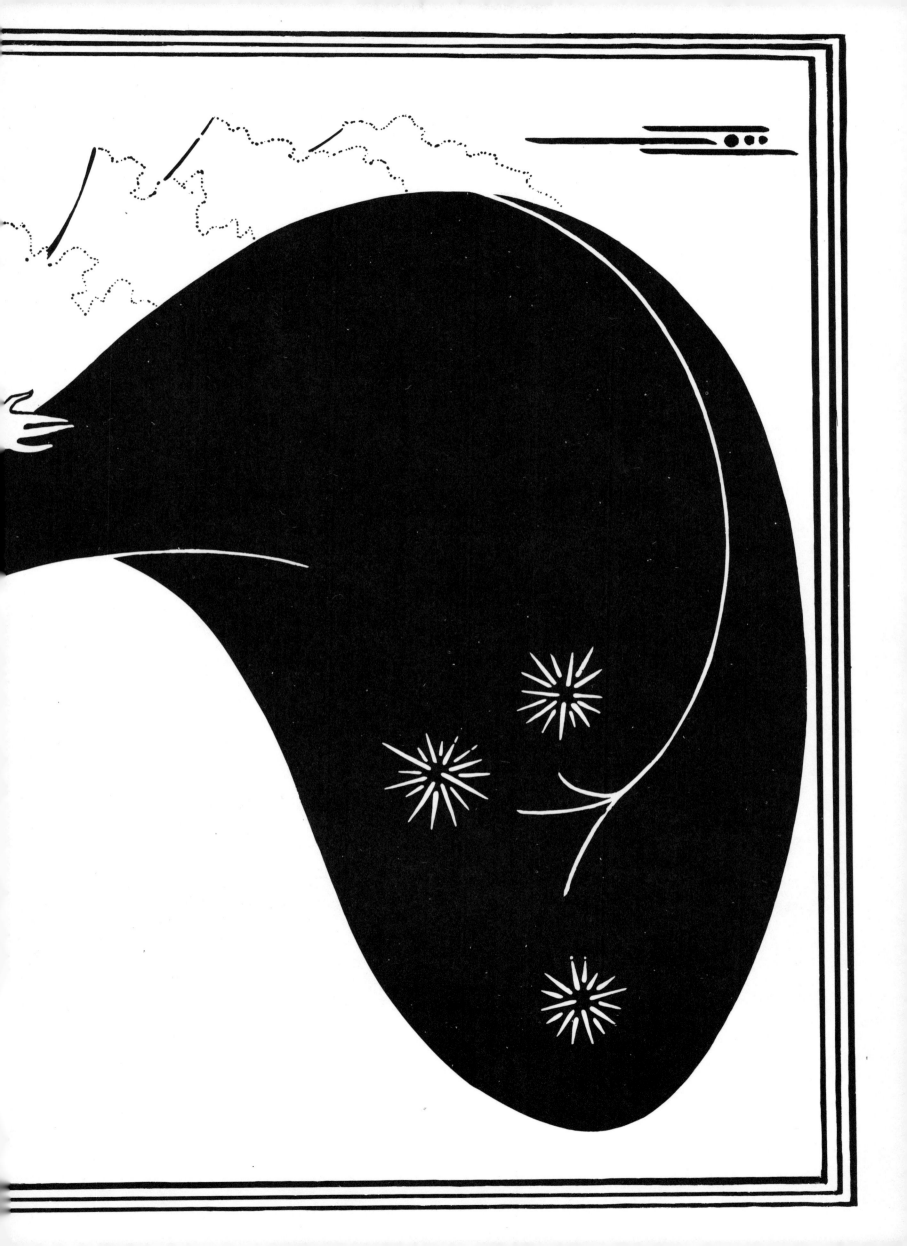

21

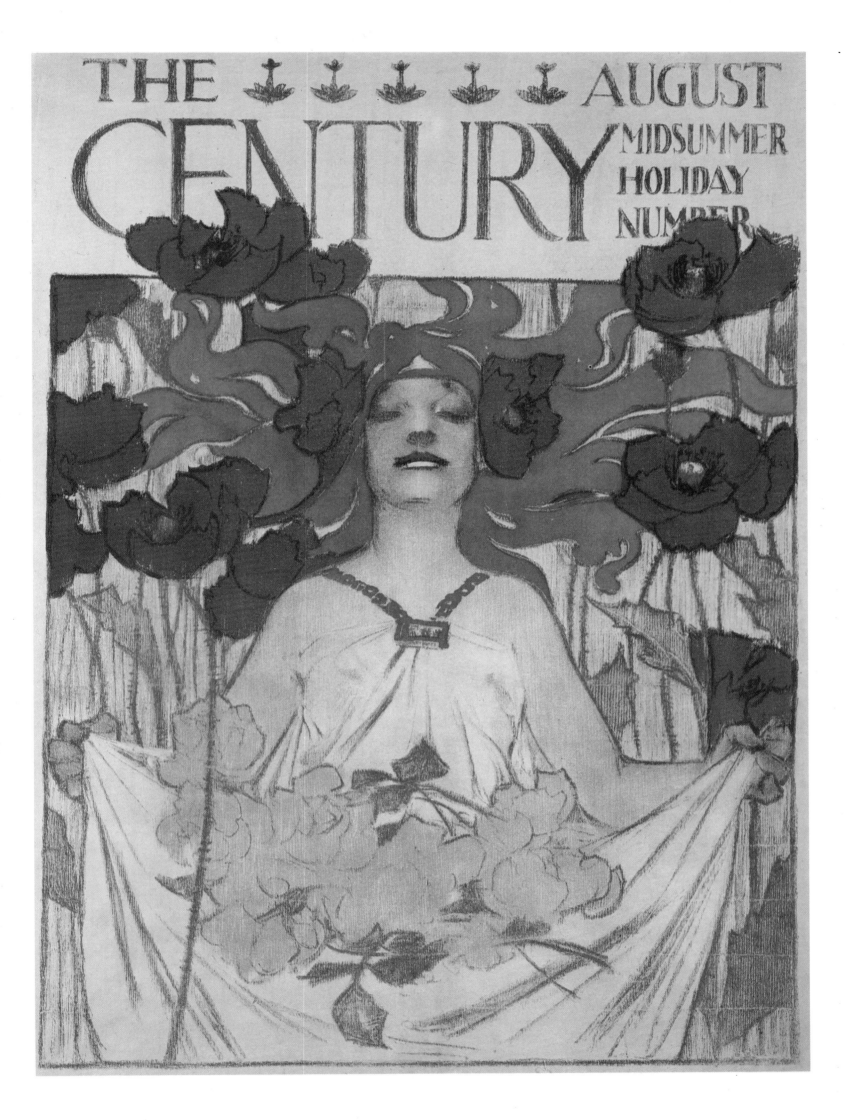

THE ECHO

Chicago's Humorous and Artistic Fortnightly

WILL H. BRADLEY

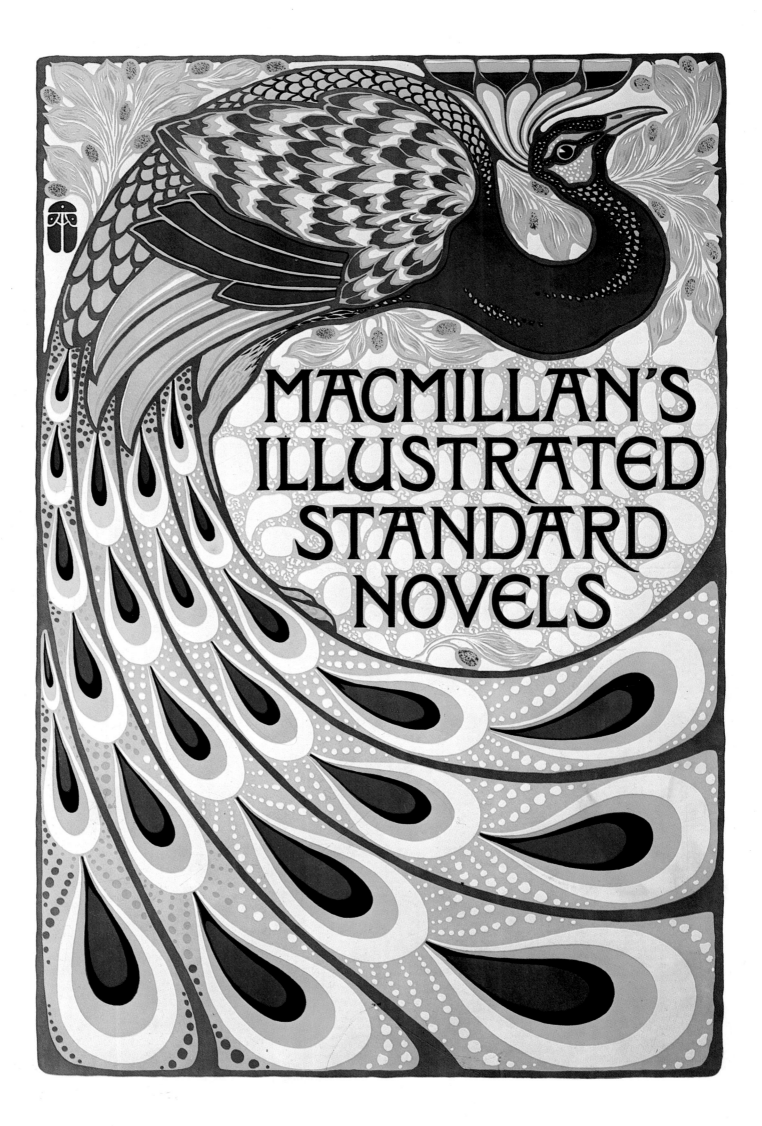

MACMILLAN'S ILLUSTRATED STANDARD NOVELS

ETERNAL·HEAVENS·AGAIN ♠ TO·FEEL·ONCE·MORE·IN
IN·PLACID·AWE·THE·STRONG·IMAGINATION·ROLL·A·SPHERE·OF·STARS
ABOVT·MY·SOVL·
YEARN'D·TO·BVRST·THE·FOLDED·GLOOM·TO·BARE·THE

Dudley Hardy

AVBREY
BEARDSLEY

Sources of Art Nouveau

Official painting in the 19th Century, as it was practised and handed down by the academies and as it was perceived by the man in the street, was chiefly concerned with representing history using the techniques which had been handed down from the great masters. The artists of the time meekly followed the classical paintings in resorting to the themes and formal ideas of antiquity and the Renaissance. This art, generally speaking, ossified into an ever more hollow mannerism which was scarcely even original. The normally oversized pictures demonstrated classical or old German pomposity in a theatrically realist manner. In Germany the leading representatives of this style were Karl von Piloty, Wilhelm von Kaulbach and Anton von Werner. A high point was reached in the pompous furnishings of von Hans Makart, beyond which there was no better image composition or artistic skill to be reached. But he was limited to a decorative reproduction of historical events. There was no new development of thought and no real artistic liveliness. Makart showed some new beginnings in his painted works, but it was left to his pupil Gustav Klimt to usher in the new age.

Just how overvalued official painting was may be demonstrated by the fact that, of the French painters of the Second Republic who were highly esteemed in their time and granted extremely lucrative official commissions, none of them was considered really important by posterity.

In economic terms the so-called 'Grunderjahre' (a period in 19th Century German history of economic boom and speculative frenzy comparable to the earlier 'South Sea Bubble' crisis in the U.K.) was an epoch of a highly successful, almost boundless capitalism.

A whole section of the population, mostly the lower middle classes, succeeded in acquiring great wealth incredibly quickly by speculating, with economic foresight and without worrying about the consequence. Possession of capital and cash profits became more important than inheritance and honest wages. The accumulation of wealth became an end in itself. "Money became a symbol of happiness and an object of desire as never before, and the invention of the telegraph served primarily to stimulate international stock exchange speculation. Riches and sorrow are the opposite poles of a bourgeois life". (Ahlers Hestermann)

It was clear, at least subconsciously, that a social crisis was imminent – a social crisis of immense proportions. Yet instead of applying themselves and bringing the influence to bear which corresponded to their position of leadership, the bourgeoisie withdrew into a pompous fantasy world.

The state enabled the parvenues to achieve an appearance which corresponded to their new status by offering peerages and distinctions which were only obtainable for money. "Riches will always display themselves, especially when they are new. Rooms were filled with sofas and chairs whose outlines were enhanced with all kinds of decorations and flourishes." (Ahlers Hestermann). Some lack of style was covered up by resorting to those fashions which had been handed down from the past. The lack of culture in the houses of these kind of people was indicative of the spirit of the age. Ornately decorated, whatever the style, the rooms were just designed for showing-off and for a primitive attempt at attaining a vain social prestige.

Rooms in the atelier style were a particularly painful display. Painters' studios of the time were stuffed full of all imaginable junk, which was potentially a source of subjects for paintings. They were more like prop storage rooms than places in which creative activity took place. Such hideous apartments, further enriched by a lumpy divan in a cluttered corner symbolised, to ordinary people, the slightly wicked world of the artist and was well worthy of imitation. Against this style of interior design, "progressive" architects worked in specific styles, Gothic perhaps, or Moorish or Renaissance. In 1876 in Munich, German Renaissance was proclaimed as the national style:- "Only when applied art and craft is established in every home can it fully and completely exert its ennobling influence on the state."

The style of painting sponsored by the Government was an analogy of this ideal. While the truly great painters of the time – Leibl, Thoma, Feuerbach – were quietly flourishing on the sidelines, the historical painters sent a wide stream of art flowing into every German home. The magnificence of the paintings and costumes and their glittering accessories was a contrast to the 'prose of daily life' i.e. the job of earning money.

In order to keep art on its fixed course, and to serve patriotic sentiments as well as to exalt the ruling house, only artists who toed the line were called to posts of leadership in the academies. Not infrequently the 'Lords of the Land' got involved to exert a corrective influence, if an unwelcome deviation appeared to threaten the teaching body. Wilhelm II of Germany declared: "An art which disregards the rules and limitations which I have set up is no longer art. It is factory work. It is a trade and must not be allowed to become art. Under the banner of that much abused word Freedom, it is very easy to fall into unstructuredness, licentiousness and self-apology".

In all the German Lander (States) there were attempts relatively early on, mostly by younger artists, to move away from official art and to create something new.

The painters of the romantic school were already open to the restless ideas of freedom and progress in art as in life. In their paintings they embodied the spirit of the age which was impinging on the consciousness of open-minded men. Revolutionary ideas found entry in a new art. Caspar David Friedrich brought a fullness of world-changing ideas into his pictures, the sort of thing which, if he had spoken out publicly would have plunged him into great political difficulties.

The intellectual elite of the time were galvanised into action by the paintings of the romantics and set on the quest for a real change of life.

Groups like the Nazarenes, who in 1809 formed an intellectual community of painters and set themselves up in antagonistic opposition to the academies, adopted even in their outer lives a strict code, which deviated sharply from the bourgeois lifestyle. They withdrew into the monastery of St Isidoro in Rome and tried to 'live for holy art' in a monastic style community. They imitated Durer's self portrait in their attire, dressed in flowing robes with their uncut hair and beards parted in the middle (called in Italian 'alla Nazereno!). They attempted to bring about a renewal of art from the spirit of the old masters.

Admittedly they were bound to conventional ideas – above all to the themes of Christian Church painting – and only managed to free themselves in the area of landscape painting.

The tendency towards living according to newly worked out norms was even stronger amongst the English pre-Raphaelites who introduced the rules of occult secret societies to their "Pre-Raphaelite Brotherhood". The leading light of this movement was Dante Gabriel Rossetti who in his art built strongly on the works of William Blake: mystical compositions filled with a rhythmic sense of movement. Apart from Rossetti it was chiefly the influence of John Everett Millais whose genius brought to bear an interesting detachment. His paintings strike one as having been painted in the 20th Century. The pre-Raphaelites took on board the Nazarenes' emphasis on simplicity and moral seriousness in art, but without the prominent religious impulse.

Rossetti painted mostly literary themes. Dante, for instance, or the search for the grail were his subjects. He managed without effort to create a link between literature and his painting. The feminine figure was always present in his pictures, whether Pandora, Sibyl, Venus or Astarte, "she is always the complete woman, at once powerful and malleable. Often she appears fateful, and at the same time, she is set opposite a different face, which is her reflection. Intensive colours and decorative elements lend her a puzzling aura somewhere between dream and reality." (Phillipe Roberts-Jones) Here for the first time, the elements which would later mark out the impressionists were coming to light.

The skill of the pre-Raphaelites in not only transporting their goals into their art, but also in formulating in words their perceptions of line and the use of space and surface, strongly affected their disciples Edward Burne-Jones, William Morris and Walter Crane.

As a painter trained in the spirit of the pre-Raphaelites, William Morris was, besides being a politician and a convinced social reformer, above all a craftsman in his main artistic endeavours. He and Rossetti's disciple, Edward Burne-Jones, produced the first typographically printed and illustrated books in 'Modern Style'. They were given an astonishingly swift and lasting distribution. Their writings especially were taken as a basis for enormous involvement in social reform. Morris campaigned for more than an improvement of the working conditions of the established factory worker. He saw beyond his material need to the clear danger that without artists participating in the expanding industrial production and supplying design, there would be a spiritual poverty of unimaginable proportions. "Machines set a new scale for the tempo of life, which had been measured for centuries by the pace of man or horse, the beat of an oar or the wind in the sails, turned fields into towns. Their iron armies created huge factories, suffocated crafts and killed off form." (Ahlers Hestermann).

The dissemination of artistically produced books was ensured by a new technological development. In 1811 Konig invented the high speed book press. By about 1850 its development had reached a standard which made possible the production of well printed books in large quantities. It was no longer just a small élite circle who could afford books. The new, illustrated books came into the hands of more and more people. Nor should the fact be overlooked that at that time a large part of the population of Western Europe was rising out of illiteracy and taking a bigger part in its political and intellectual development.

Morris's special interest was in typographic renewal – the creation of carefully produced books. To this end in 1888 he opened his own printshop, the Kelmscott Press. Book decoration and illustration improved in quality and popularity enormously during those years. The range of themes for illustrated books also increased. In this context we are indebted to Walter Crane for a novelty in the history of books. He produced picture books for children and thereby created a completely new kind of book. Apart from his activity as a painter and illustrator he also wrote many theoretical works on the problems of book production, which were very influential.

There can be seen in the work of these three people the intellectual and practical beginnings of Art Nouveau, as well as an essential part of the theoretical basis of the new art. Creative seriousness, combined in their artistic designs and their science of book-graphics with a complete faithfulness to their materials, had an enduring influence on the further development of Art Nouveau. Their aim was artistic complexity, a union of art and life in which all men could take part. This end would be served on the one hand by aesthetic training, and on the other hand by the craftsman's purity in all his activities. Morris realised these ideals with consistency, including setting up Socialist communal workshops in which furniture, cloth and utensils were carefully and artistically produced. The firm of Morris, Marshall and Faulkner became the starting point for Art Nouveau arts and crafts.

In a similar manner the young impressionists provided impetus for and acted as a source of reform. Unperturbed by the hostility of the public and the ignorance of their colleagues at the Academy they were beating a path away from the traditional classical painting. They discovered the independent strength of pure colour. They accorded colour the highest value in relation to light and space, with an absolute disregard for the theme of the picture, which according to the traditional view was supposed to be the actual point of any artistic activity. Impressionism dispensed with everything that up to then had brought popular success with the audience: content, ideas and sentimental or moralistic imagery. It proclaimed the theme of the picture to be completely irrelevant. The external masks, flickering in the light, the atmosphere was what they wanted to portray. The realisation of impressions became the goal of painting. One group of painters – their spokesman was Seurat – dispersed their painting into single dots of paint, set close together, similar to modern four-colour printing. This technique, which went into the art-history books as pointillism was built on correct theories of physical perception, but could never satisfactorily create a picture. This perception very quickly found some of the impressionists losing the substance behind colourful glittering surfaces, and the pictures that came out displayed a drastic shortage of structure. Painters like Renoir began, by using firm lines, to bring back a sense of design into their paintings. Yet it was not until Cezanne that the style succeeded in bringing impressionistic effect of colour into accord with clear composition. Van Gogh and many other young painters learned from him. A transformation began amongst a certain group of impressionistic painters and these artists built on perceptions which were bestowed on them by Art Nouveau.

Western artists also received stimulation from an extremely different stream of cultural development. From the Far East, especially from China, there had already come to Europe in Rococo a powerful cultural impetus. At that time unusually fine artistic works and crafts held sway in the ruling houses of the West. Expensive porcelain, silk carpets, lacquerworks from the Middle Kingdom: such were the decor requirements of Rococo residences. The Far East was always an important element in the world of 19th Century decor. However, Japanese coloured woodcuts from Hokusai, Hiroshige and Utamaro, which were first shown at the Paris Exposition of 1867, were a sensation. In Japan itself, such woodcuts were treated as folkart and were of relatively little value – in any case they were certainly not thought of as high art. In the West, however these works were like a beacon fire.

After the forced opening of Japanese ports by American warships in 1853, the previously closed country quickly began to orient itself politically and economically toward the West. Japan henceforth took part in the expositions and brought not only porcelain and craft items, but above all, very large stocks of 18th Century woodcuts onto the Western market.

The sovereign relationship with space, without artificial shadow or perspective depth, the elegant control of line and the consequently unified composition fascinated the young band of questing artists in Paris. The enormous colourfulness, the quality of printing previously unknown in the West, and not least the great freedom of choice of theme, all excited them. The principles of production of Japanese woodcut art were easily understood, so many artists brought the liberating element of the Eastern art into their new works. Without the intervention of the Japanese woodcut into Western art, the creativity of Art Nouveau would certainly have turned out differently – poorer and more cramped.

The same Samuel Bing whose gallery in Paris gave its name to Art Nouveau had a shop, founded in 1871, also in Paris in which he sold art products, especially woodcuts, imported from Japan. He also published a journal called *Artistic Japan* which was sold in a parallel German translation in Leipzig as *Japanischer Formenschatz* (Treasures of Japanese Form). In yet another respect Bing brought a new element to the Paris art scene. He was the first to get to know the works of Louis Comfort Tiffany and the new line in American Art Nouveau graphics, and to introduce them to Paris.

Symbolism was a further current in the plastic arts which was a development away from traditional painting and led to Art Nouveau. The symbolists sought their themes in areas which had little or nothing to do with the surface of human life. Symbolism was the visual expression of a literary and intellectual movement with a completely different kind of influence. Its themes were based on dream, magic, sleep, the fantastic. Death and beyond, hallucination and visionary mysticism were the sources of this art, in which the absolute precedence of spirit over matter was sought.

In contrast to impressionism, which was purely an artistic movement, symbolism developed out of thought and dream. Discussion was the basis and heart of this art. Out of discussion came painting or poetry. This close relationship between poets and painters was – at least in France – exceedingly successful.

The official art of the period was still merely a pompous reflection of a stern materialism which held sway over all of civilisation. Poets like Verlaine, Rimbaud, Maeterlinck and Verhaeren kicked against it. Painters like Moreau, Redon and Puvis de Chavannes followed them and brought forth their visions as pictures. They set themselves against the economic and technical trend and brought into their work the precedence of the spiritual over the physical. They nobilised all the strength that animated consciousness. They viewed the world as imagination not inspiration.

"The realism of Courbet and the landscape painters of his school, just like Monet's impressionism, rejected fantasy and set themselves the goal of only representing reality. In the full light of one, and the half darkness of the other, subjectivity was lacking, however great the sensitivity of Sisley and Pissarro, however generous the vision of Monet, however passionate Manet may have been." (J. Cassou)

The basic symbolist poets were Baudelaire and Mallarmé. The movement's spiritual founder in Germany was Nietsche. He considered that man's art was an opportunity to raise a brief moment of desire on the long road to death by lending him a little drunkenness and madness.

Precursors of symbolism – in part also sources for the Nazerenes and the pre-Raphaelites – included Goya, Blake, Fuseli and Turner. Turner was, in his search for a representation of atmosphere, a forerunner of the impressionists, and he widened the path for the symbolists. He was not simply concerned with the effect of light; the imaginary also found access to his work. His later painting completely rejected reality in favour of a fantastic vision.

Fuseli's works were strongly under the spell of the expression of inner tension and erotic dreams. Blake, on the other hand, was a visionary. In his work he tried to create a junction between the eternal and the temporal. In his paintings he gave earthly form to his perceptions of supernatural worlds. Goya ended up fleeing the horrors of war and withdrawing into the world of his own ideas of force. The Symbolists built on the foundation of all these four. Their work meets us everywhere as the starting point for symbolists in Art Nouveau.

Two phenomena distinguish the development of Art Nouveau from other modern art movements. Firstly the explosive speed with which the style came to the consciousness of many artists, and more so of the general public, was astonishing. Secondly, it always had a strong bond with applied art and especially with crafts.

When one sees what a troubled path the artists of impressionism and expressionism had to walk to see their works no longer dishonoured and rejected, but understood, it is bewildering to see how the Art Nouveau movement was accepted and became ubiquitous in daily life within a few years.

There is a close connection between the many applications of Art Nouveau and its dissemination. The realm of crafts was especially open to new forms. The first world exhibition in London's Hyde Park in 1851, which was to advance the fame of the British Empire and demonstrate progress in many fields, showed, hidden under all the pomp and circumstance, an unprecedented qualitative decline in craft exposition. It was evident that form was at its most pretentious and that art was simply a sort of processing with no regard to the materials used. A new spirit simply had to arise; form and ability had to be brought into action again. So the way was cleared for a willing acceptance of the new style. The nascent shift to industrial production and the concomitant mass production also helped to spark off a quest for something new in arts and crafts.

Because of the positive acceptance of Art Nouveau by all circles of the population, commissions were offered and executed in the new style. Thus when Paris's first underground was built in 1900 the commission for the new staircases in the stations was awarded to the architect Hector Guimard in the "style moderne". So an audience of millions, the whole population of a major city passed Art Nouveau objects on their daily journey to work. As would not be the case in styles of art which are restricted to painting and sculpture, Art Nouveau could invade all areas of public life precisely because of the many uses to which it could be put.

The connections of representative art with Art Nouveau are many, and on many levels. The interpretation on the stage as an important factor will be referred to again. Without the world of cabaret in Paris and other expressions of the demi-monde the graphic work of a Toulouse-Lautrec would be unthinkable. The singer Aristide Bruant and his Ambassadeurs Theatre survived in Lautrec's powerful posters. Dancers like Loie Fuller, with her metre-wide flowing veils, inspired artists from all over Europe. Jules Cheret, Thomas Theodor Heine, Will Bradley and Kolo Mauser, among others, dedicated charming graphic works to her dancing skills. The actress Sarah Bernhardt was in the works of Mucha the standard bearer of a whole style. Even the name of May Belfort would probably be unknown to us if the works of Art Nouveau artists had not given her the breath of immortality – and if she in turn had not inflamed the painters with the skill of her performances.

In the area of serious music it was mainly opera that provided stimulus. Can one seriously doubt, when one looks at Beardsley's illustrations of Wagner, that Wagner inspired the great graphic genius. In the same way the music of Richard Strauss and Gustav Mahler inspired the artists of the Vienna school.

The most lively combination and the richest in interaction was between the entertainments of the cabaret (poetry, song, dance, acting) with the painters, sculptors and other artists of Berlin and Munich. Von Wolzogen's "Uberbrettl" (Superstage), set up in 1901 in the Berliner Art Nouveau building ("Buntes Theater"). The name Superstage was inspired by Nietzsche's 'Superman' and was more literature orientated, so its effect on Art Nouveau was limited. In Munich on the other hand, "Die elf Scharfrichter" was firmly settled at the centre of artistic life. The singer Marya Delvard became the 'trademark' of cabaret, portrayed by Heine in a skin-tight black dress. And in Kobus' 'Artists Pub' in which the cabaret "Simplicissimus" was produced, the list of co-workers and regular guests reads like a who's-who of Art Nouveau culture – "Heine, Gulbransson, Thony, Reznicek, Wilke and Schulz gathered there and frequently paid their bills with drawings which were the main attraction of the pub!" (E. Pablé).

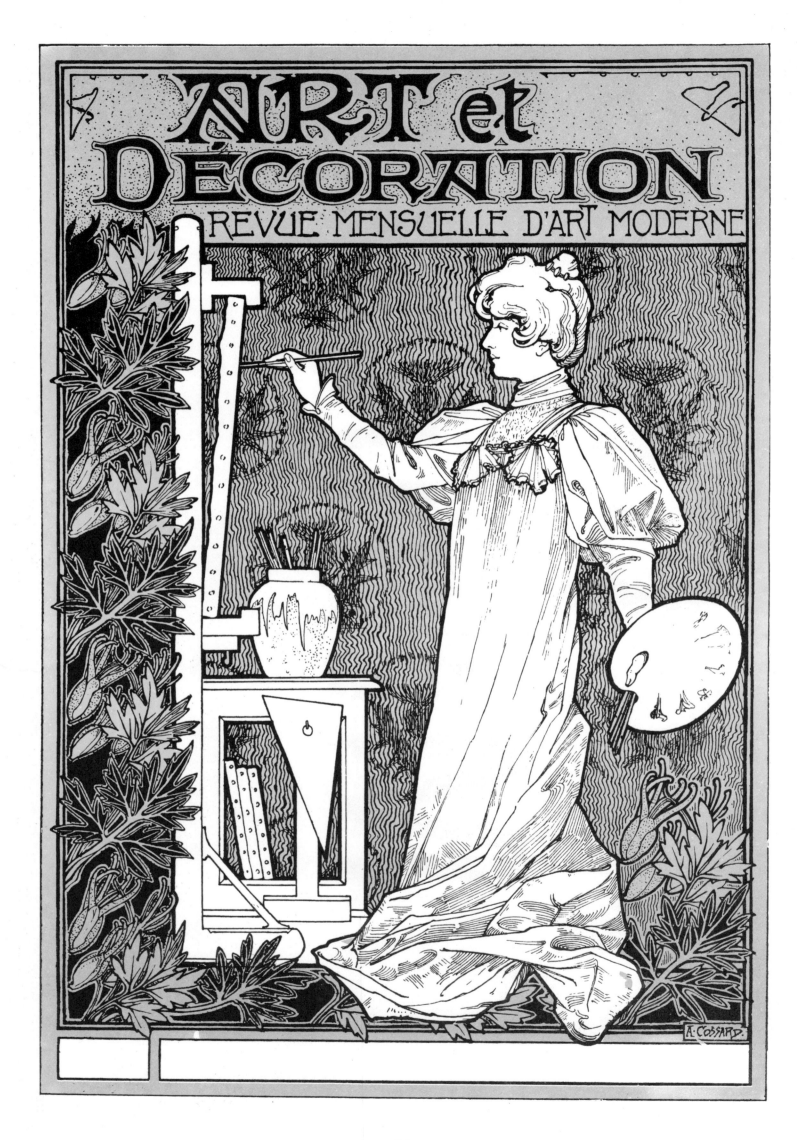

Imp. CHARLES VERNEAU, 114, Rue Oberkampf, PARIS (Deposé)

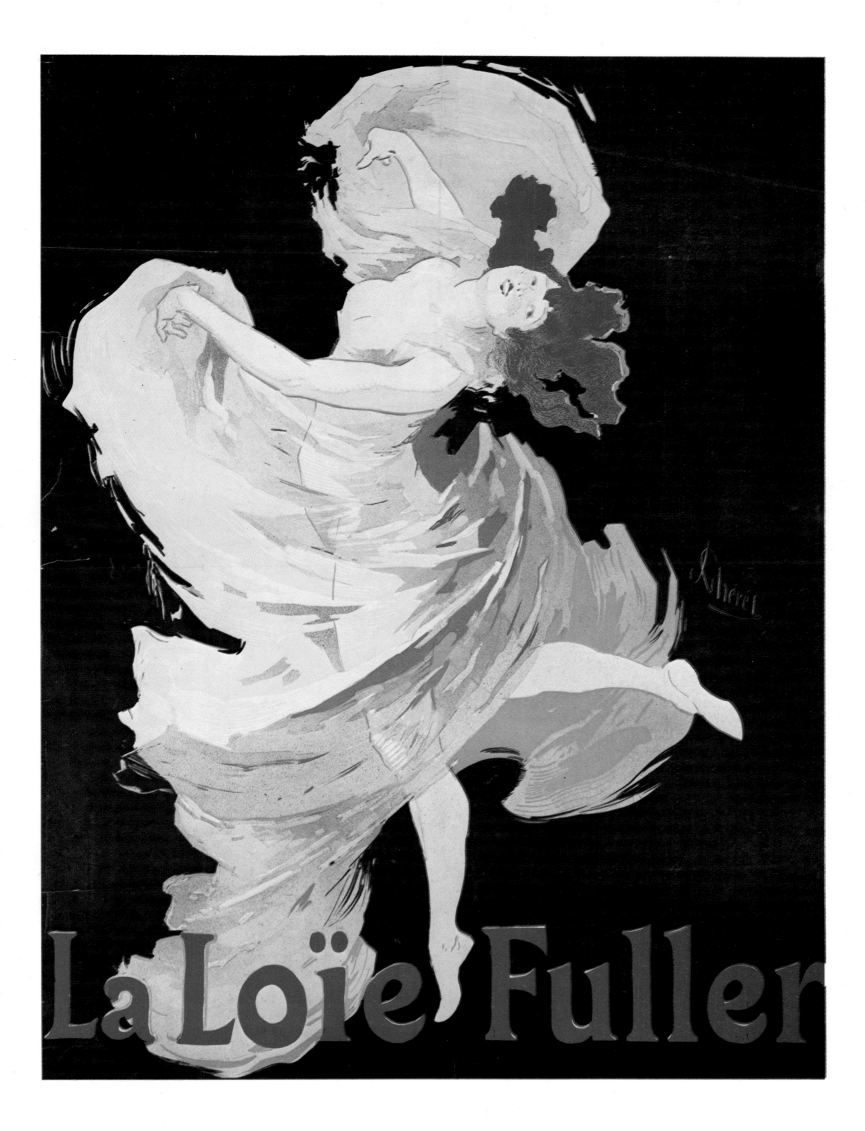

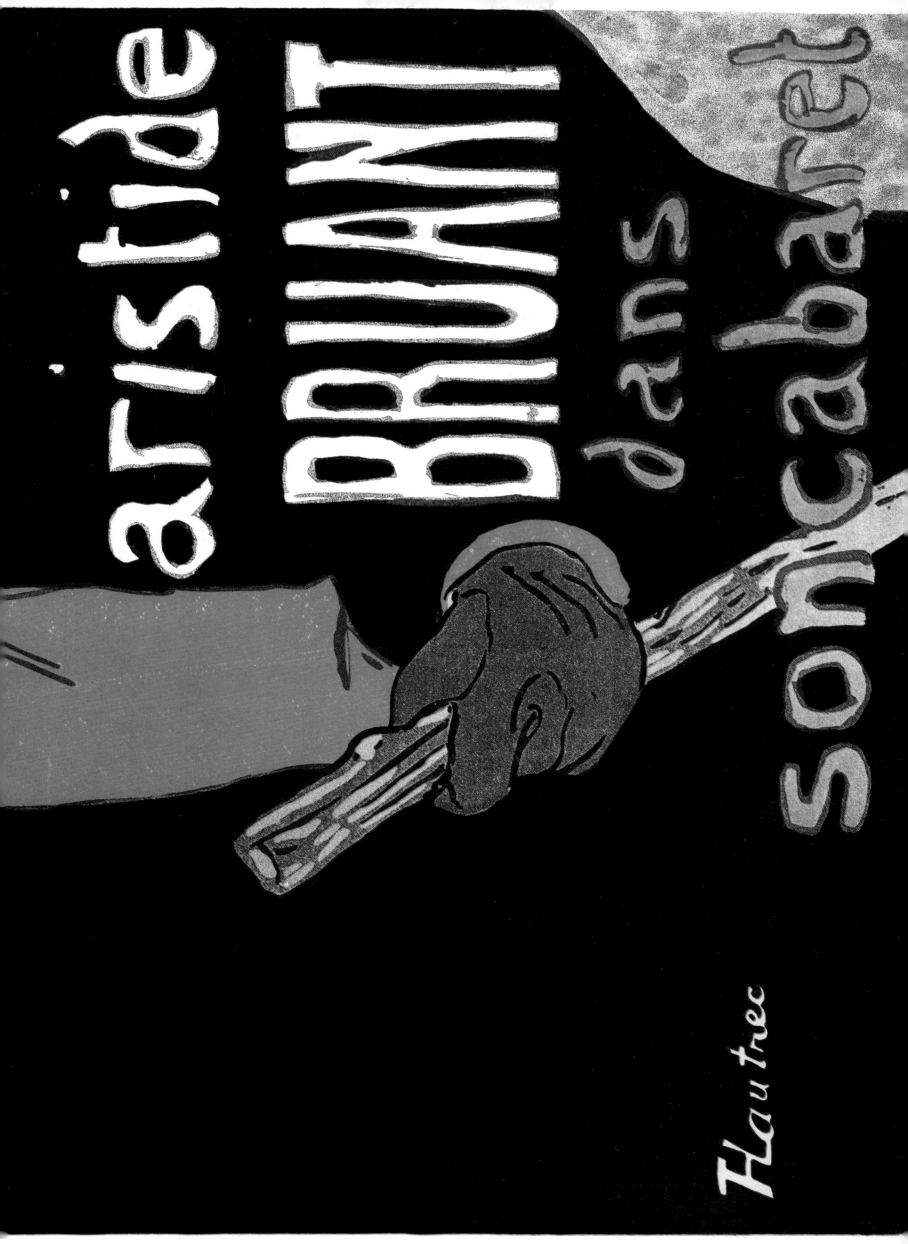

Mucha
Willette. Léandre.
Steinlen. Vogel.
Huard. Calbet de Feure
Doës. Villon. Wibop. Roubille
Verbeck. Burret. Muller. Vély etc.

Directeur Paul Boutigny

Rédaction Administration 9 Rue Say Paris

en vente partout le Numéro 30 centimes

imp CHARLES VERNEAU 114 Rue Oberkampf PARIS

History of Art Nouveau Graphics.

The taking up of Art Nouveau ideas, and the transposition of those ideas into work, began at quite different times in different European countries and with differing intensity.

In France there was a current of 'unofficial art' which was completely open to the new style. In Germany the new trend set in substantially later than the analagous movements in her Western neighbours. But in England the new style began from craft-based assumptions that had been prevalent there for decades.

The previously mentioned innovation in the area of book production around 1850 had results in another field: journals. Here was a wide range of potential for literary, topical and illustrative self-expression. Graphic art was adopted eagerly by the editors as a vital medium of production, which meant ad hoc publicity for the artists concerned.

An important journal of the time was *The Yellow Book*, and the artist who achieved ovrnight success with it was Aubrey Beardsley. By nature oversensitive and thin-skinned, he suffered in his early years from consumption which eventually took his life in pitiful circumstances at the early age of 26. He sought refuge in a dandyish appearance, so that his weak constitution and his tender temperament provided him, so to speak, with a protective cover. It is beyond doubt that Beardsley shocked his countrymen toward the end of the exceedingly prudish Victorian age. It is also certain that there were circles in which he was esteemed precisely because of his perversity and decadent spirit, and that the sudden appearance of his exalted works could register a certain amount of success on the sensation factor alone.

His singular talent and that perfect stylistic completeness which showed in his work from the start are of a stature which makes him unique. From the first moment he stepped onto the stage of art – and he certainly treated art as a stage – he was complete; without the possibility of improvement, but also without flaw. He obviously learned the sovereign treatment of space and line from the Japanese, but his precise work put them completely in the shade. He had a scarcely comprehensible blend of contrasts. Caustic satires, and icy eroticism, a cool, nervous, unbelievably precise stroke made up one side of his work. Sweeping movement of line, the almost sick hand of coquettish costume and ecstatic inspirations of romantic-symbolist content made up the other. *The Yellow Book* was co-funded by him and lived on his graphic invention. Nevertheless the journal eventually had to be suspended for economic reasons. Its successor was *The Savoy*, published by a successful London antiquarian who specialised in erotica.

Another English art journal of great importance in the spreading of the new style – in other countries as well since this publication came to the notice of people on the continent and provided stimulus for native journals – was *The Studio*. It had been appearing in London since 1893. The activity of this organ was not limited to critical asides on the revolutionary artistic endeavour. It was supportive and provided many illustrations as examples.

Apart from the high speed book press, there was another technical achievement that was of decided importance for Art Nouveau graphics. Lithography, invented in 1799 by Senefelder, had reached such a level of development that in England large format colour printing became possible. Although the machine and the technical knowledge was developed in England, leading artists of the country at first kept away from the new technology. In France on the other hand, the new colour printing fell on fruitful soil. The painter Chéret had learned the art of lithography in England and created the first colour revue posters. Toulouse-Lautrec likewise immediately adopted the new printing process and his first production was a gigantic and powerful poster for the Moulin Rouge. The delightful technique suited his graphic generosity and the audacity of his lines. Fired by Lautrec's sensational success, Chéret then applied the full force of his well-founded lithographic ability. There followed a kind of poster-war from which all Paris benefitted.

In order to understand the excitement of the public over the new posters one must realise that in the 1890's the colour picture simply did not exist in those miserable gray streets. There were only monochrome text posters in the most naive layouts and the concept of advertising was still completely in its infancy. Suddenly there was this outbreak of colour, power and pert frivolity. With the demand of advertising space suddenly appearing out of nowhere, the Berliner Ernst Litfass came just in the nick of time to erect his poster-pillars which were named 'Litfass-pillars' in his honour. Now the gaily coloured posters were at the centre of attention in the boulevards. Art Nouveau graphics became famous overnight. Paris was caught up for years in a whirl of posters.

There was almost no brand of performance art which did not use posters to invite potential customers to theatres, music halls, concerts, dance palaces and ice rinks. All sorts of goods were suddenly advertised. And it did not take long for the art dealers and collectors to recognise the value of the posters as works of art. Today one finds posters in many graphic collections which have been carefully peeled off pillars. There were also at the time several large reproduction firms who offered posters to an exclusive audience of collectors. These posters were freshly printed, often smaller than the originals, and frequently without the text of the original advertisement.

A large number of artists devoted themselves to the new art. Toulouse-Lautrec and Chéret were the most important but Théophile Steinlen was no less successful. His posters specifically contained an element of social criticism. While Chéret cultivated the pert elegance of his female forms in ever new varieties,

Lautrec sympathetically portrayed the hateful element in human nature and in a decaying environment which was only rarely brightened by a breath of warmth. Steinlen was the artist who laid bare, and complained. Chéret's world was a healthy one; Toulouse-Lautrec's was sick; Steinlen fought for a better world.

Chéret brought the techniques of colour lithography to its utmost perfection. He had learned the trade of the lithographers in England and, on his return to Paris, opened his own lithographic establishment. One noticed in his work that he drew the design on the stone with his own hand. By that action, he raised lithography to an original artistic process that was particularly suited to posters. His pictures of elegant Parisians, scantily clad girls, and dancers or singers from the "Cafes chantants" were called "Les Chérettes" by the public. These women, dressed with great chic and moving so gracefully, were the epitome of Parisian taste.

The work of the Swiss artist Eugène Grasset, who had been living in Paris since 1871, had a great influence on the use of the poster. Grasset was an architect who came by way of book production and crafts to the poster. His intellectual origins in the pre-Raphaelites is clear. His art was a model for Will Bradley in America and for many artists in Germany.

Just as popular as Chéret was Alphonse Mucha, a Czech living in Paris. In France his works carried the description 'Style Mucha' and were widely imitated. Mucha's favourite theme, in almost all of his works, was woman, whom he represented as a puzzling dream figure. With one poster for the actress Sarah Bernhardt in the role of Gismonde he came instantly into vogue. He was enormously busy as a poster artist and scarcely less so as a jewellery designer.

His recognition as a painter suffered a little because of his popularity as a graphic artist. This upset Mucha throughout his whole life, for he was at heart a painter.

The first artistic poster with class that was published in England to great acclaim was Fred Walker's "Women in White" in 1871. It was an early example of Art Nouveau. Beardsley's work did not follow until twenty years later and by then enthusiasm for the modern poster was common. In the same year the first designs of the Beggarstaff Brothers appeared, a pseudonymn behind which were hiding William Nicholson and James Pryde. Their works with the simplest materials and abstract designs were never surpassed, nor was their influence on poster art.

John Hassall and Dudley Hardy were particularly versatile and much sought after. Hardy played the same role in England as Chéret in France and was a master of the delicate hand. His posters for *A Gaiety Girl* at the Prince of Wales Theatre made him world famous. They were reproduced in all the journals as especially good examples of posters from the London theatre scene.

France and England stood as godparents for the poster art of America. Louis John Read got to know the work of Grasset in Paris in 1894 and on his return home devoted himself entirely to poster art, achieving great popularity within a few years. His posters pointed the way for the artistic poster in America. The posters of William Bradley were no less successful. He was not just a poster artist; he actually made his name as a book designer, typographer and illustrator. In this area his influence on European book art can be seen. He set new standards with his journal *Will Bradley: His Book*, for which he was editor, poet, author and printer.

In the field of book decoration, and of illustration in books and journals, great advances were also made in France in the last decades of the 19th Century. While in England it was only a small circle who adhered to the new art and sought to realise the new spirit in their own work, in France there were a great number of artists whose graphic works tended towards Art Nouveau. The key role which Gauguin played in introducing Art Nouveau to painting will be discussed in the chapter on painting. One journal in particular was important for graphics: *La Revue Blanche*, with artists like Bonnard, Vuillard, Vallotton and Toulouse-Lautrec. The editorial staff also included Henry von de Velde and the Norwegian Edvard Munch.

Of this group Vallotton, a Swiss living in Paris, was of the greatest importance to Art Nouveau graphics in France. No one had achieved such results as he with the juxtaposition of black and white to indicate the presence of opposites. His woodcuts, with their cool surfaces and the contrasts of black and white as sharp as a cast shadow made him so famous that people almost forgot that he was primarily an oil painter. When he felt that he had completely exhausted his experiments with black and white he immediately had done with them and turned wholly to his painting. Hausenstein wrote in 1918 about Vallotton's *Baigneuses*, 'If a style is as enormously strong as the style of this woodcut vignette then it is more than a book illustration, it is the standard bearer of the taste of a generation, present and future.'

In Germany, magazine production became a rallying point for graphic artists. In Munich the journals *Jugend* and *Insel*, and the illustrated humorous journal *Simplicissimus* appeared, and in Berlin, *Pan*. In all these publications, new strength was active, pressing for a new arrangement of the artistic situation. *Pan* had a Hamburg man to thank for its graphic format: Otto Eckmann, who found for the journal a formal expression which came to be called aristocratic. He used stylised flower and animal motifs combined gracefully with purely linear ornamentation. His frames and vignettes have a plain but noble effect and display no frivolous ornamental playfulness. Eckmann's script is today still considered the classic Art Nouveau script.

The editors-in-chief of the journal were Julius Meier-Graefe and Otto Julius Bierbaum, the poet. By his international editorial contacts Meier-Graefe "brought the world into his house" so that *Pan's* horizons encompassed its homeland and beyond. However, the financial framework of the exquisitely and expensively designed journal brought its own problems. The partners in the concern were nearly all representatives of German high finance who naturally wanted to lead the journal on a somewhat élite course. So Bierbaum soon withdrew from the editorial staff. He did not think that the journal would last long under those conditions, "Because it rested on an overvaluing of the German bourgeoisie. Apart from them, you can't find 1000 people in favour of the developing art. *Pan* was the journal of the millionaires; a journal you don't read, but leave lying on the parlour table when you are entertaining people of taste and intellect – in that, it will already have achieved its purpose".

The style of the journal *Jugend* which first appeared in 1896 was quite different. The administrators of *Jugend* took an easy stance straight away, feeling themselves simply to be editors, and leaving the illustrators to their own style, though admittedly the logo by Ludwig von Zumbusch appeared as a beacon and took shape in Hirth's slogan 'Let Jugend be the banner!'

Hirth was an experienced publisher. He had already obtained considerable knowledge of editorial and production skills with his incredibly successful "Formenschatz" (Treasury of Form), an extensive collection of graphic designs. His *Jugend* could now offer something new, for he had found a way of printing parts of the journal in colour which led to a powerful effect from a distance and significantly increased the attraction of the graphic works. *Simplicissimus* also quickly adopted this new graphic process.

Jugend became a real reservoir for Art Nouveau artists, without being the actual mouthpiece. It was never opinion-forming, but offered opportunities for artists to work in the new style. It aimed to shake off the boredom paralysing the magazine sector both in terms of pictures and literature. "Jugend" the word was a programme. More than that! It was a fanfare! It only needed to be spoken, written, painted, lived! It embodied joy and rebellion, charm and cheek, hope and fulfilment. (A. de Nora) The *Hamburg News* wrote: "*Jugend* of Munich has conquered the world in the short time it has existed. It has all the properties of a conquerer: spirit and strength, impudent daring and divine cheek; it is beating on the thick heads of the Philistines, turning a forceful nose up at pedantic learnedness and academic pathos. It laughs and jokes about intolerance in art and life. It stresses the firecrackers of its jokes on the worthy pates of mean-spirited pedants."

A few months after the birth of *Jugend, Simplicissimus* was founded in Munich. This journal devoted itself completely to humour and only occasionally dealt with Art Nouveau. Its content was limited to a narrow circle of themes and there was among the editorial staff a perennial fear that the readers would get tired of the continuous repetition of the same jokes. *Simplicissimus* had a certain strangeness to be sure but this had nothing to do with art. Its humour was particularly irritating to the authorities and consequently the state prosecutor was a frequent visitor on account of lèse-majesté and similar offences. To dodge arrest, publishers and editors frequently worked from abroad. But even prison sentences could not reduce their sarcasm. It survived until the Nazis killed it.

The third of the Munich journals *Insel* (Island) was produced by two cousins who came to Munich from Bremen. Alfred Heymel and Luddof Schroder wanted to realise a long held dream of their youth. They got Otto Julius Bierbaum involved following his departure from *Pan*. Heymel's considerable abilities made it possible to produce the journal in an especially beautiful form with a high standard of printing. Committed to an editorial programme of "regenerating the German mind, *Insel*, was an expressly literary publication. However it is its few illustrations which are of importance today. Apart from Heine, who was also attached to *Simplicissimus* and *Jugend*, it was the young Markus Behmer who stood out with his admirably drawn distorting fantasies. Any kind of journalistic or economic success worthy of mention was denied to the paper. Published by Heymel for three years under great financial difficulties, it finally went under because of a complete lack of public support. In spite of that, it was the foundation of the world famous Insel Publishing Company. Heymel had an extraordinary building designed and built for him by R.A. Schroder which for years was a literary meeting point. It prompted Heine to say "Goethe could have died here". There is a story by Heine that shows the joie de vivre among artists during those years. "Everything was outrageously tasteful. The food was served on old Meissen china with real gold cutlery, which was silver-plated in order to avoid any reference to the parvenu. We spoke continually of Goethe and felt that we were very exclusive. We couldn't bear it any longer! Something had to happen. Deciding quickly, I brought a piece of meat up to my mouth with a knife. Alfred Kubin who sat opposite me shouted 'Heine has eaten with his knife, yipee!' He jumped up and executed a wild dance with Saharet who up to that point had been classically bored next to Heymel . . ."

The illustrated book was of great importance in Germany and as a novelty Albert Langen introduced the picture cover with Art Nouveau motifs to his books. To be sure there was the danger that the production of a book would kill off the content. "The beautiful book was in 1900 more talked about than the good book. In many cases the illustrative and decorative qualities of the book were more important than its content or the style of its author. A shift in accent from the book as literary art to the book as graphic art is detectable". (Simon).

Stanley Weintraub handed down an anecdote about the joker Oscar Wilde and Ada Leverson: she suggested to him that he should bring out a book which contained only marginal decorations. It should be full of beautiful unwritten thoughts, made out of Japanese paper, and expensively bound in Nile-green leather, and should be a limited and numbered edition, a work of art, very rare!

Wilde agreed. "It will be dedicated to you," he told her "and the unwritten text will be illustrated by Aubrey Beardsley. We will need five hundred copies for our good friends and one for America."

The extremely talented artist Theodor Heine provided in 1897 a typical example of decoration superseding content. He illustrated *Die Barrisons*, a book issued by the publishers of *Pan*. This was a thrilling example of Art Nouveau in book art, a monument to production with a completely insignificant text about the most popular Revue girls of the time. Heine also produced pictures for *Pan*, but was best known for his book covers, designed for Albert Langen, and for his drawings for *Simplicissimus*. He was one of the liveliest and most exciting illustators of Art Nouveau. He remained faithful to Simplicissimus until the rise to power of Nazism in 1933 forced him into immediate exile abroad, having become one of the most hated of journalists. He died in Stockholm in 1948, well advanced in years but also highly honoured as an artist in Sweden.

J.R. Witzel had a special kind of genius when it came to the art of line and space. For him the end of the page was no limitation for he cut into the edges of his drawings with such power that the viewer automatically brought in the space beyond the drawing.

Another artist deserves mention: Baron Hans Henning Voigt who worked under the pseudonym of Alastair. Clearly under the influence of Beardsley he created a decadent in fin de siècle style to which he remained faithful during his whole life, and which brought him international recognition.

The tendency towards erotica in Art Nouveau was fostered by many artists in Munich at the time. For example, Franz Bleis Publications for a short time published a journal with erotic works. So did the journal *Die Auster* (Oyster) whose chief artist was Franz von Bayros. All these publications were accessible only to a small circle and were distributed in limited editions with small print runs.

The transcendence to symbol – this will be dealt with in greater depth in the section on painting – is a phenomenon that meets us in the Art Nouveau graphics of Austria. Artists don't worry their heads over what symbol and allegory mean, but it is without doubt that they had great and holy thoughts to express and were sure that their ideas would unlock the secrets of nature. Their world was an ideal world, higher than daily life. Here as elsewhere (in painting) the transcendence to symbol was new in the works of Bocklin or Klinger or Stuck or Knopff. To them the abnormal was universal, the philosophy more important than the individual.

Ver Sacrum (Holy Spring) was the title of the journal of the Viennese secession as well as the manifesto of the artists, the password to art in their country at the time. Viennese artists around 1900 wanted to lend their art plain and frank expression; they wanted to guard truth and preserve beauty through their work.

There arose an expressly Austrian and Viennese art. The city offered a completely unique intellectual climate for development. As unforced gaiety brought artists together in Munich, so in Vienna it was psychoanalysis which did not arise in Vienna out of nothing. The psychoanalysis of Freud fertilised the whole of intellectual life. However, it was not a science independent of the problems of daily life but was bound up with the needs and concerns of the people of its time. That it arose, could arise, and had to arise in Vienna, characterises the spiritual condition of this metropolis which was on the one hand transparent and on the other hand clothed its suppressed longings in symbols. The world of Art Nouveau imagery fed wholly on this world.

Secession, founded in Vienna under the auspices of "The Union of Plastic Artists of Austria" became a reservoir of all the country's creative powers. At the same time it concerned itself with contacting like-minded people in other countries. Its mouthpiece was the journal *Ver Sacrum*. Predominantly it was artists of the Art Nouveau style who formed the editorial staff of the journal. It developed an extremely strong independent style built up of geometrical and ornamental components. "We want an art that doesn't bow to foreigners but which neither hates nor fears foreigners. Foreign art should stimulate us to think for ourselves. We want to recognise them and admire their worth, but we don't want to copy them." So it was written in the first issue of *Ver Sacrum* and it really did succeed in this area, bringing to Vienna impressionism and symbolism, Japanese art and Northern art, Segantine, Hodler and van Gogh, Cézanne and Seurat together with works of the artists of Austria itself.

In 1903 another union of artists appeared on the scene. They were to an extent the same people who had previously carried *Secession* but who had walked out on account of differences of opinion. Now they got together to form the *"Vienna Workshops"* which also achieved noteworthy success in the realm of graphics. Their distinguished head was Gustav Klimt, an important painter who also left behind a large number of graphic works, noted for the independent character of his drawing style. This style of hand-drawing was carried on by his disciple Egon Schiele, who quickly developed away from his master as a painter. Under the heading of Graphics must also be mentioned the young Oskar Kokoschka and his work for the Vienna Workshops. He and Egon Schiele built bridges between Art Nouveau and Austrian expressionism.

ZOOLOGISCHER GARTEN MÜNCHEN

EINTRITTSPREISE: FÜR ERWACHSENE
KINDER UNTER 12 JAHREN

60 Pfg.. AM FREITAG Mk.1.-
20 Pfg.. AM FREITAG 30 Pfg.

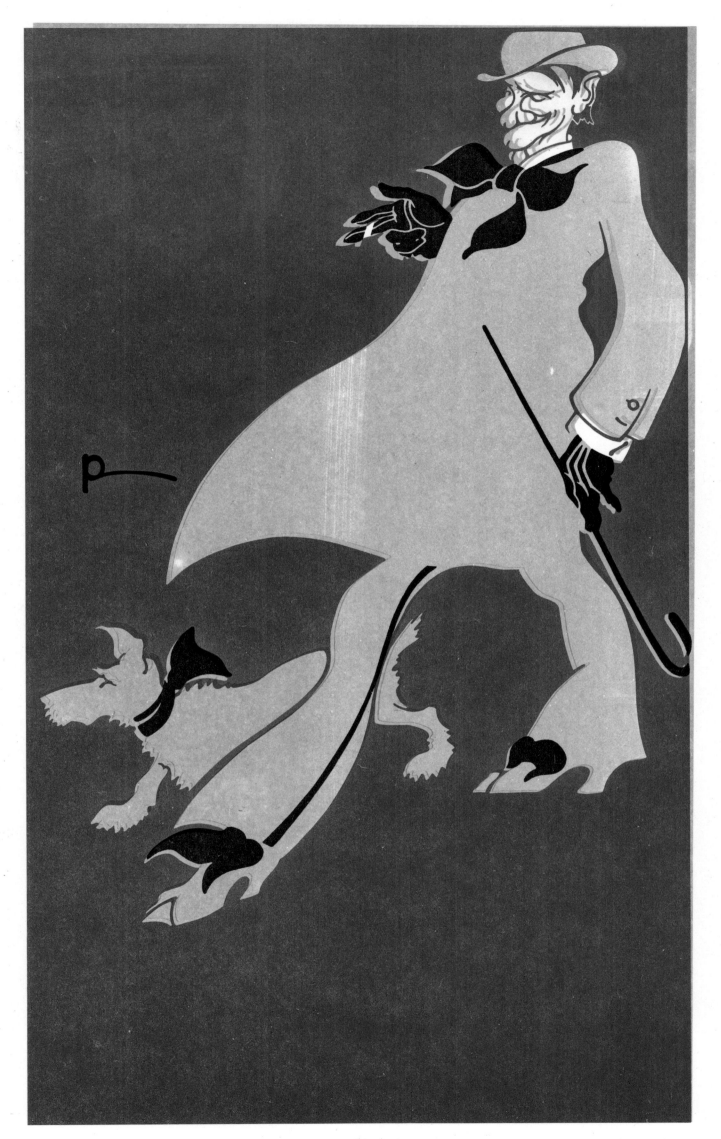

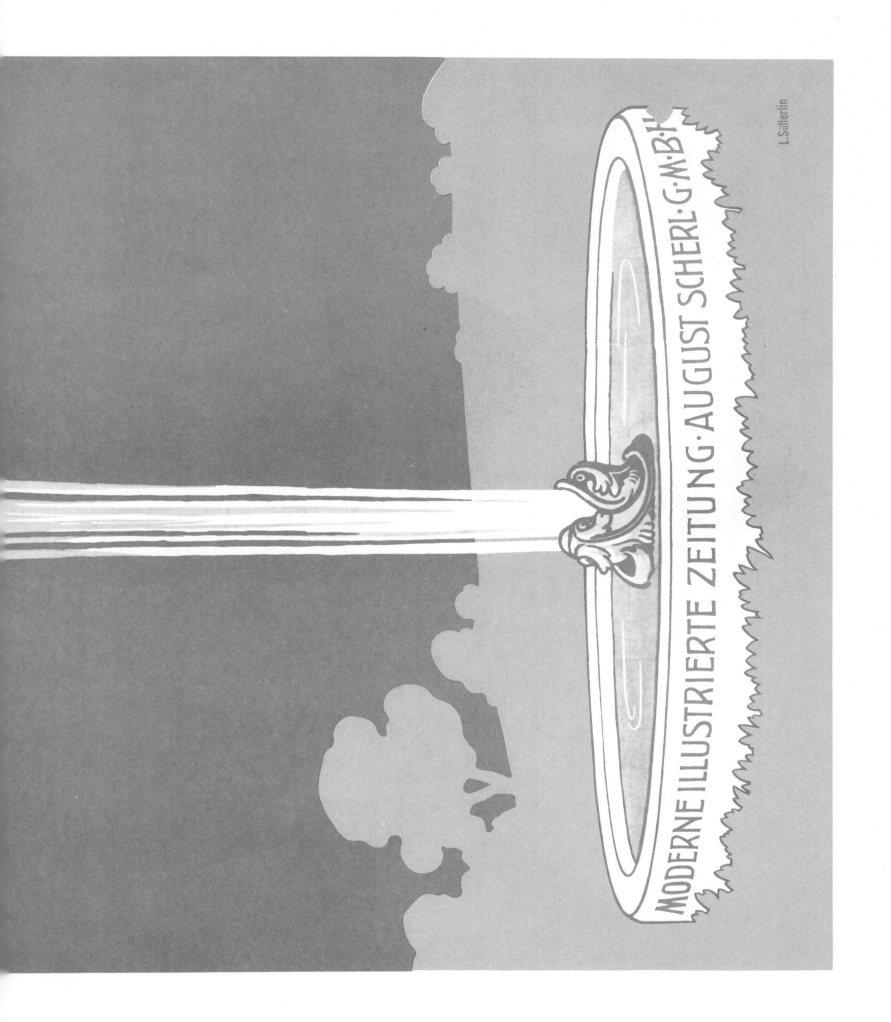

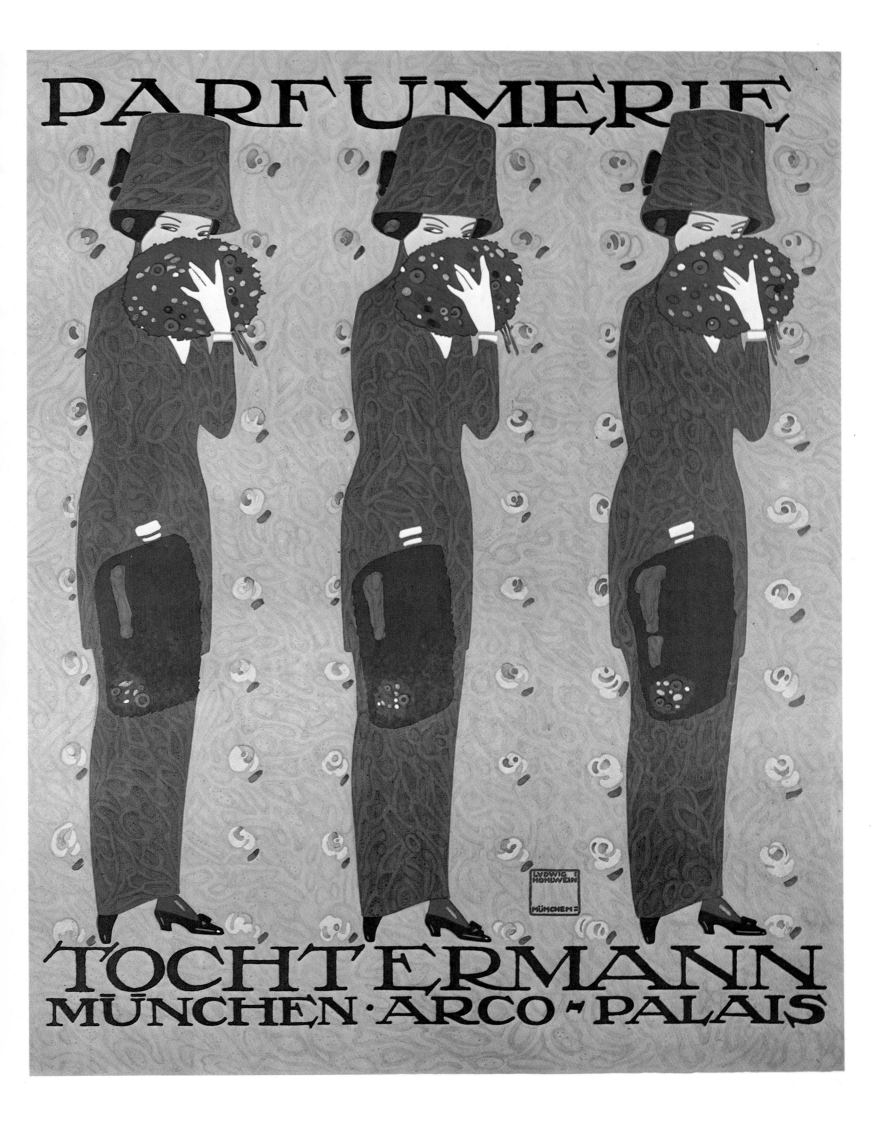

101

Münchener Scharfrichter

VEREINIGTE DRUCKEREIEN & KUNSTANSTALTEN GMBH (6XHUR & G.) MÜNCHEN

109

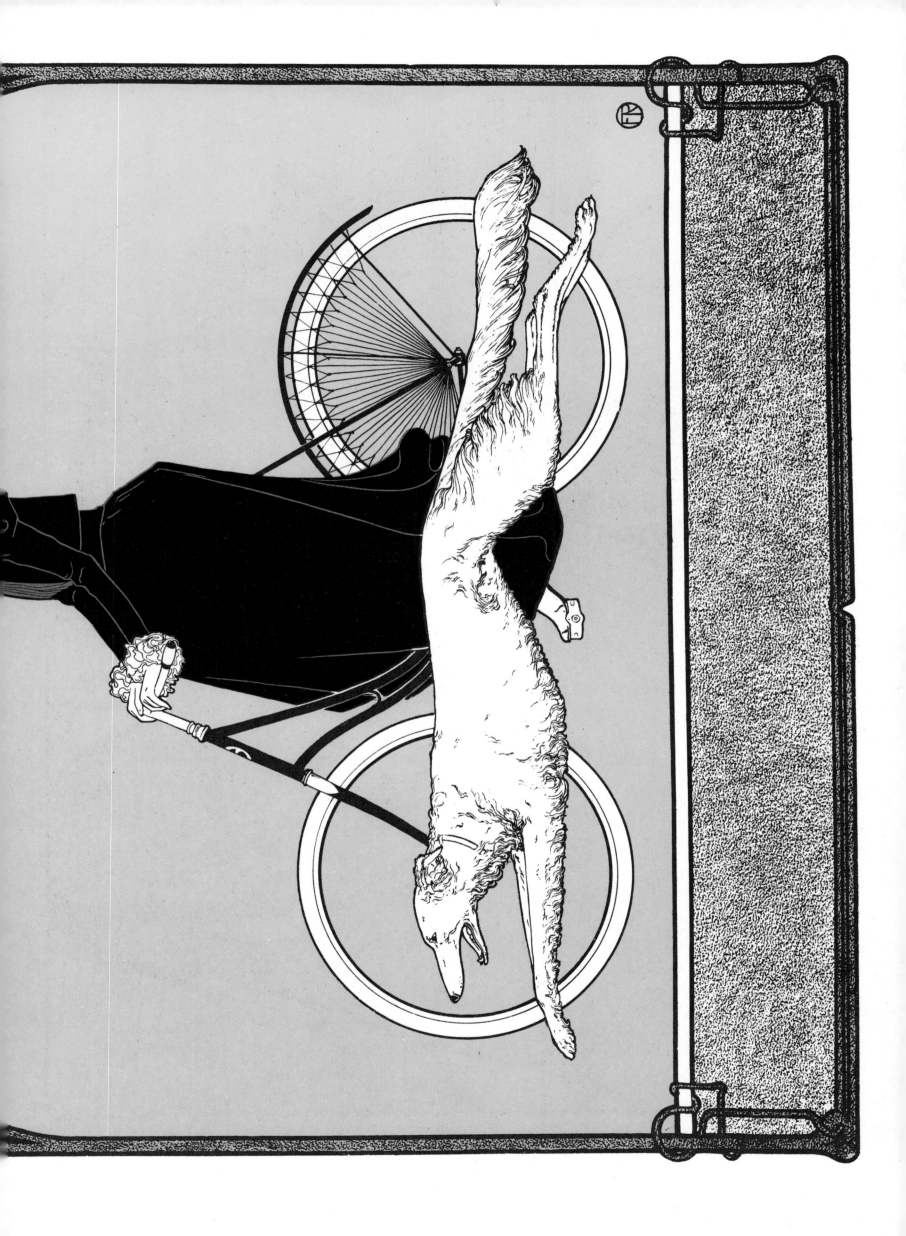

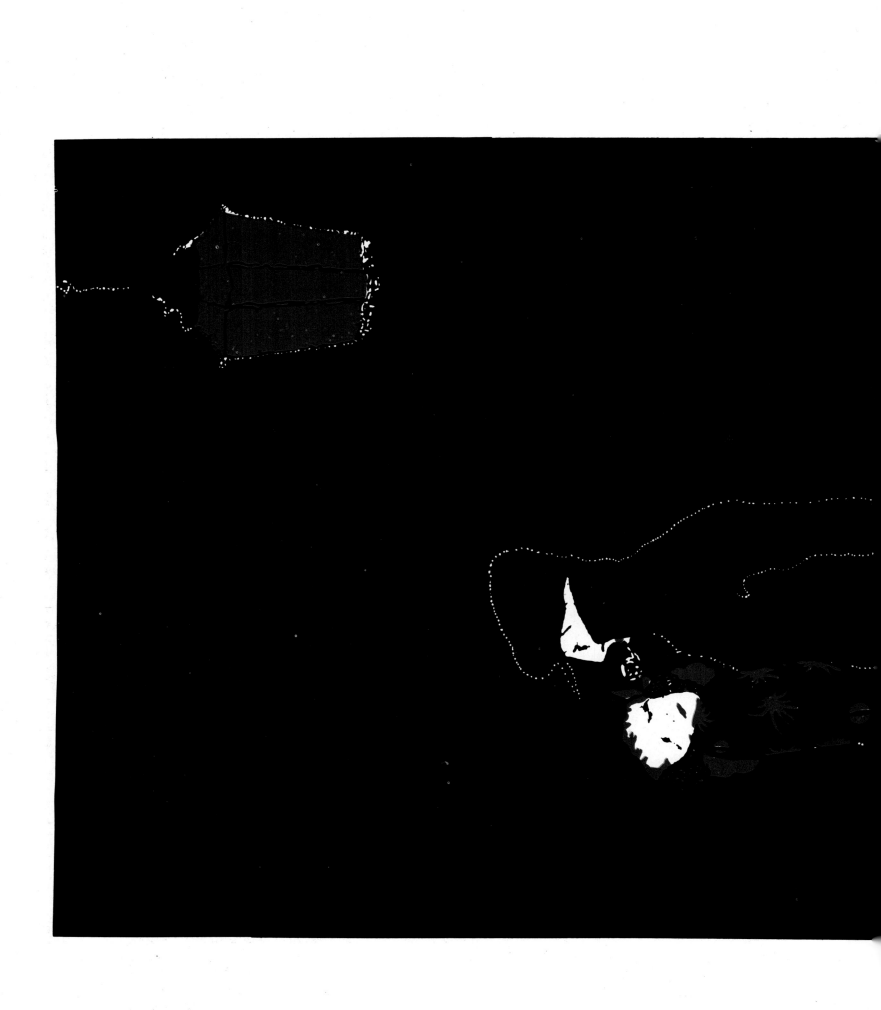

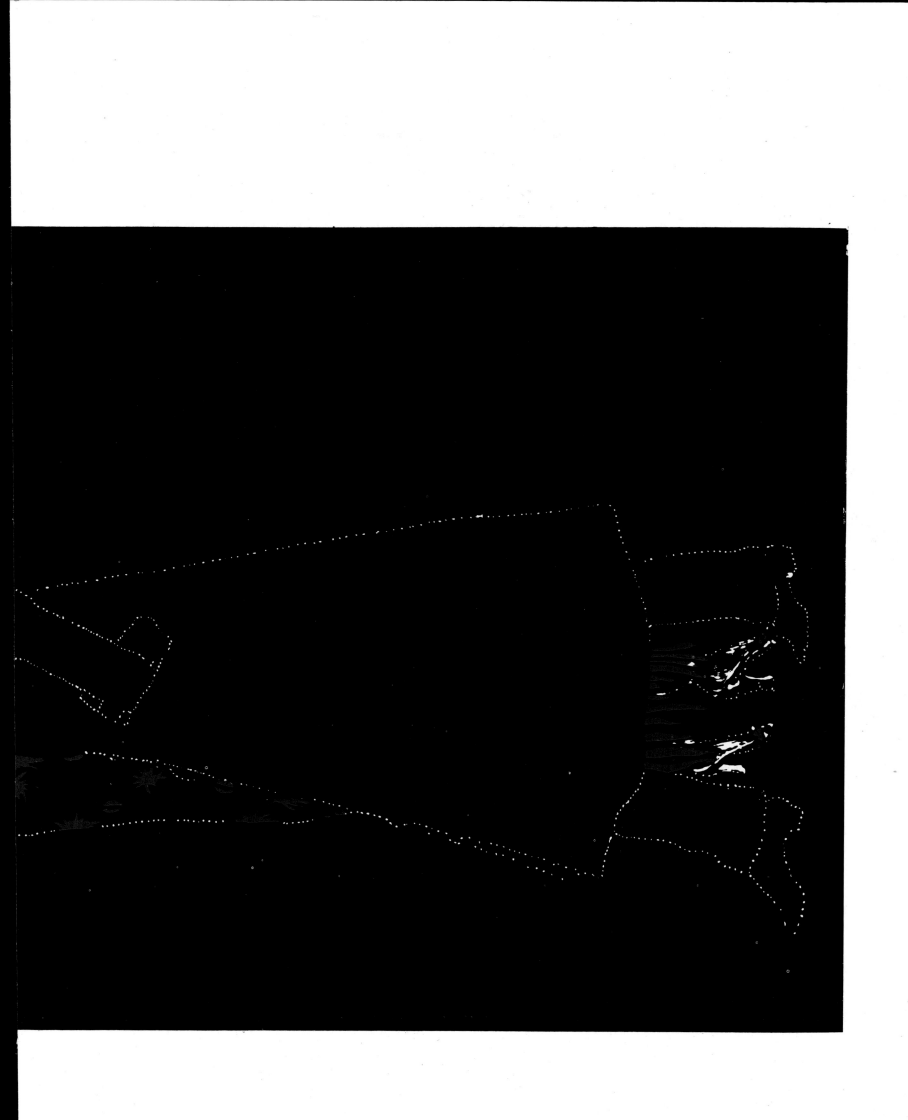

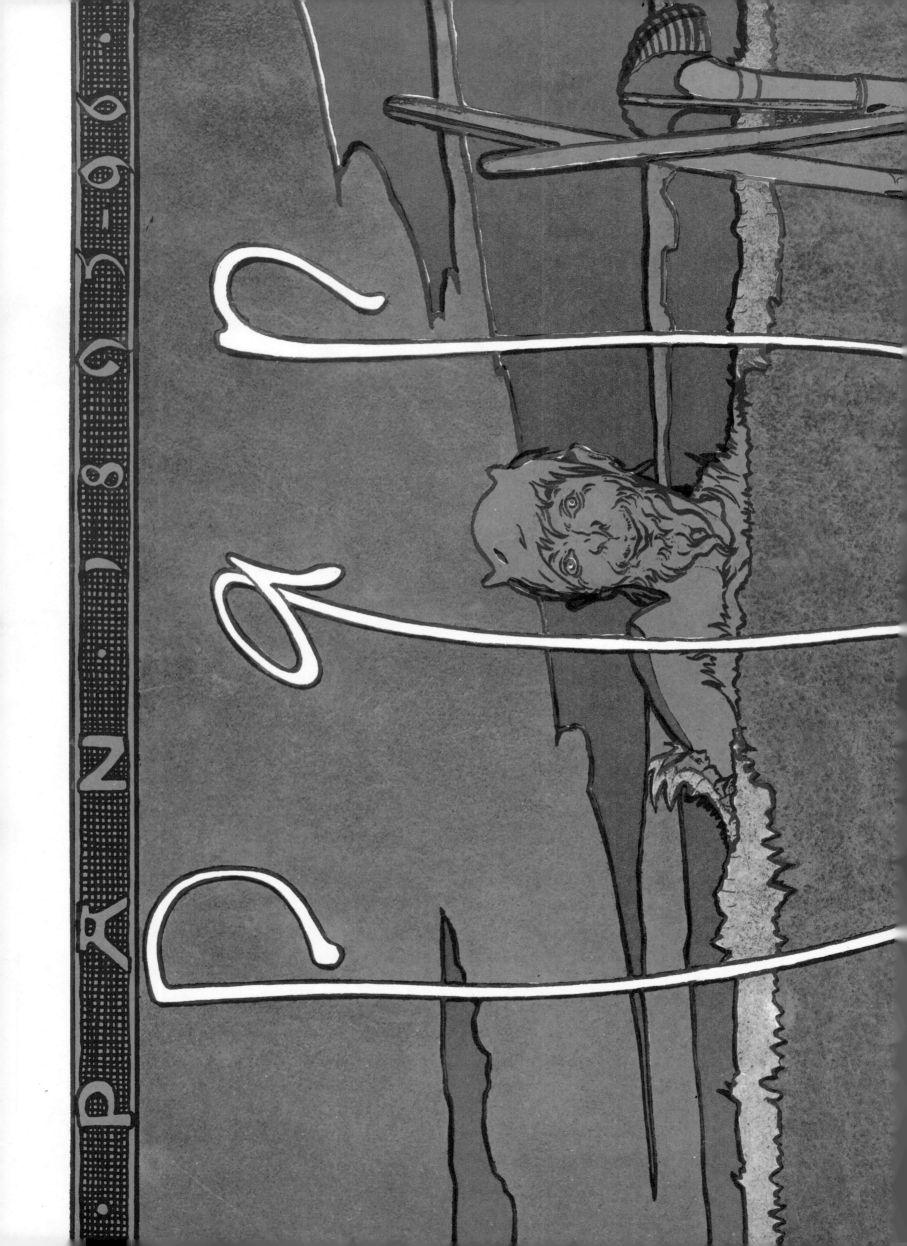

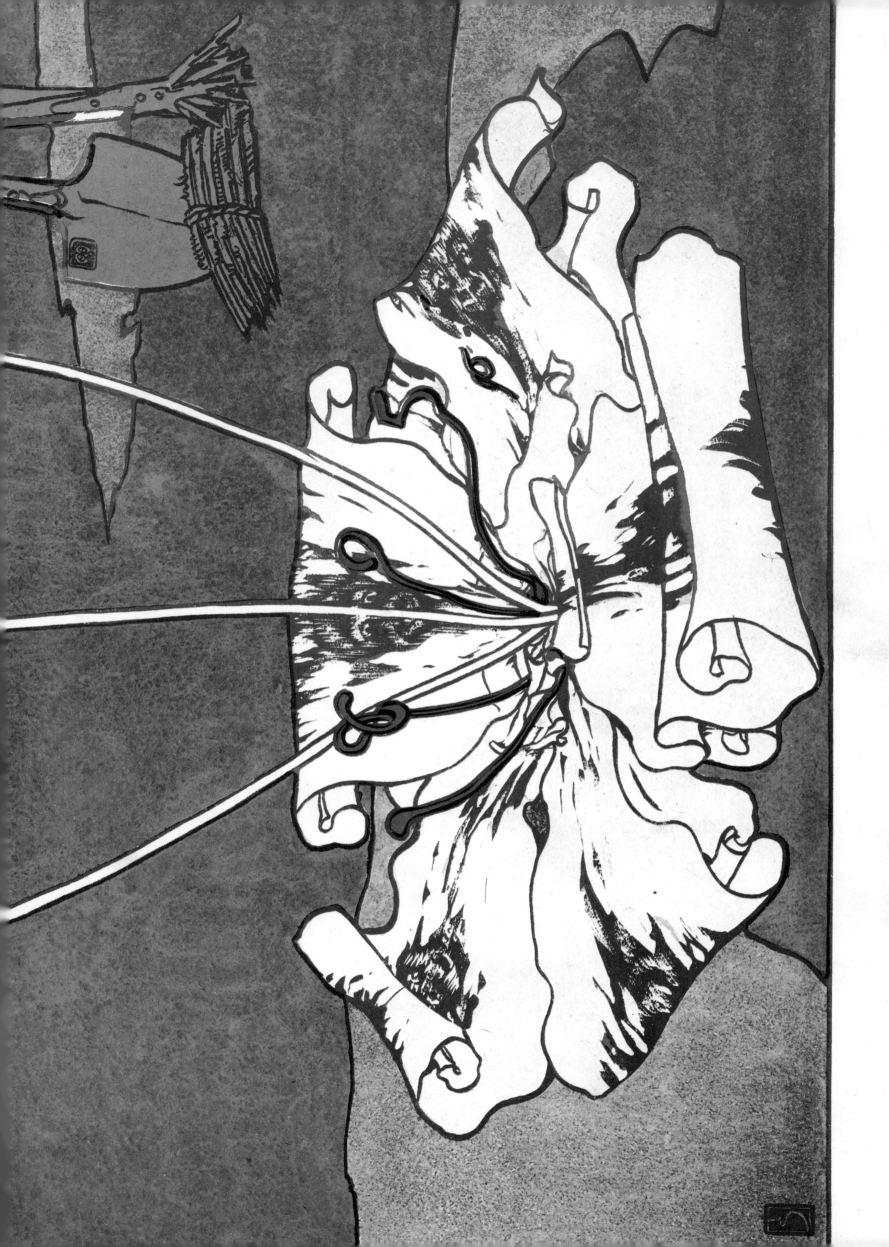

Art Nouveau Painting

It is a remarkable fact that Art Nouveau was enormously successful in the field of applied art and conquered with amazing speed all areas of life where form and design were necessary. In painting however the role of Art Nouveau was weaker. It gave a powerful impulse for artists to set new goals but at first only a few aware individuals made this departure. Out of their individual acts they formed a movement which pushed back the senescent art of yesterday into the lumber-room. Yet Art Nouveau remained for many artists a passing phase, a way-station in their life's work.

For a long time even art historians could not decide whether to treat Art Nouveau as a uniform, recognisable trend. According to Hammann, "relationships to painting can be seen only in isolated cases. Moreover they are unstable relationships. The characteristics of the style arose for the art trade, and it is only with the benefit of hindsight that one can see it transferred to certain manifestations of painting. . . . . . so when we speak of Art Nouveau in painting, we are speaking of only an outward and formal relationship."

One can recognise, however, especially in French painting, continuous lines of logic, that lead painting styles into Art Nouveau, and dovetailed seamlessly into the development of modern art.

In the chapter on the sources of Art Nouveau we looked at the derivation of Art Nouveau via Romanticism and William Blake to the pre-Raphaelites and on to Walter Crane. In France, feeding on these sources, symbolism developed, built on strong literary foundations. Its main representative was Gustave Moreau whose lascivious female figures impressed other symbolist painters. Moreau like historical painters, sought his themes in the Bible or in mythology. He then gave them new or double meanings with ideas and symbols, which produced a completely new image content. Moreau's pictures exhibited a magnificent personal style. His works were the result of many studies which he finally combined with an orientally dreamlike decor in a whole composition. His female figures are confusing: 'symbolic divinity of indestructable voluptuousness'. The seductive femininity of the figures combined in the decor with an utterly unbelievable colourfulness. 'The colour must be thought, dreamed, imagined', he once said. The Swiss Arnold Bocklin also belongs to the early stages of Art Nouveau. His female figures stand together with those of Moreau. He also painted archaic landscapes in which he embedded his ambiguous symbolism. Most of his paintings are overshadowed by a deep and dangerous melancholy.

The central figure of symbolism was, however, undoubtedly Odilon Redon, who at the same time stood closest to Art Nouveau. 'I think I have submitted myself docilely to the secret laws which led me, for good or ill, to build things out of my dreams, as well as I am able, in which I laid my whole ego'. With this sentence he described the heart of his art, in which he tried to realise the unreal in mystical colouring. 'I suppose my whole originality lies in the fact that I allow improbable beings to live like men according to the laws of the probable by putting, as far as I can, the logic of the visible in the service of the invisible'. Redon brought symbolism into Art Nouveau. He knew and used the colours of impressionism of which he availed himself thoroughly for use in corresponding themes and became the champion of a symbiosis which seemed to have grown out from him.

Paris was a crystallisation point for the new art. There, all the forces gathered which had hitherto sought to comprise an undercurrent against official tastes in art. In Paris the new style built on this foundation and radiated out from there into all European countries and to America. The years 1860 to 1880 were a time in which many artists sought and experimented, found new things and also altered things. Older artists took up the 'Modern Style' as a new and enlarging element in their later work. Young artists often started off in the Art Nouveau style although they changed it in a short time by developing it further.

Above all, however, the upswing out of impressionism became a fruitful source. From the beginning of the 80's more and more artists took the trouble to give their pictures a new form and a firmness of composition. Edgar Degas, Auguste Renoir, and above all Paul Cézanne began in their landscapes, with reasoned design of figures and themes, to give their pictures space and the composition a clear structure. Finally Van Gogh and Toulouse-Lautrec, grouped together as a younger generation than the impressionists, grasped eagerly at the liberating use of colour but promptly subordinated it to their own desires and to their inner moods. Together with Gauguin the two painters took the path from impressionism to expressionism, and other artists, among them Bonnard, Vuillard and Maurice Denis aligned themselves with their perceptions. It was the painting of Gauguin in particular which prepared the way for other painters because, as distinct from the works of Van Gogh and Lautrec, his pictures had a great universality. He displayed commonly held perceptions and did not make them unrecognisable under his individual hand. Along the way from impressionism to expressionism, Art Nouveau came into considerable importance. Out of Art Nouveau came Ornament; the liberating movement stemmed from there. Then came the particular loosening of line and surface which flowed into the artists' work out of the Japanese woodcuts, first into their graphics and then also into their painting.

At times one of the acquired perceptions gained the upper hand, which led to paintings especially rich in tension. A good example of this is seen in the work of two Duchmen. Jan Toorop Bilder created pictures with symbolic content by the application of a quite extreme technique that used impressionistically intensive colours which he learned from the Japanese.

The second Dutch artist was Jan Thorn-Prikker, who began as an impressionist painter, but then helped himself to a too-rich and very bitter style, also under the influence of the Japanese. Thorn-Prikker devoted himself later especially to the symbolic representation of Christian themes. The renewal of Christian art in the 20th Century owes a lot to him.

Art Nouveau was limited to a short lifespan and some rudimentary beginnings in a few pictures by young artists like Picasso, Matisse and Braque, who came to be considered as the Fauvist Group. Matisse was strongly impressed by the rhythmic element of Art Nouveau, while Picasso, as was the way of his genius, sipped at the chalice of Art Nouveau, contributed a few arabesques, and then turned his restless artistic curiosity to other things.

Art Nouveau became important as a kind of liberation to the Norwegian Edvard Munch. As he totally absorbed the new colour of the impressionists, so he was gripped by the liveliness of his own colleagues who were just then moving away from impressionism with the help of Art Nouveau elements. The French tried to give their art fresh expression through a new cryptic conception of objects, while retaining the impressionists' palette. From the beginning Munch tended towards themes which precluded an emphatic painting such as that of the impressionists. Stimulated by the young French artists, he added to his work a strongly expressionist tenor.

On his return to Norway he devoted himself to themes with a symbolic character: he painted works such as *Puberty* and *The Kiss*. Munch's *Dance in a Summer's Night* could well stand alongside the works of Bernard, who painted with Gauguin. With his great, drifting contours, he gave shape to the secret of life, the subconscious demonic impulses, the oppressive loneliness. He succeeded like no other, combining seamlessly in his important expressionistic works the colour of impressionism and the liveliness of Art Nouveau.

Art Nouveau painting in Germany was essentially confined to the same cultural centres that also took the lead in crafts and graphics: Munich, Berlin, Darmstadt, Karlsruhe, and Worpswede. Admittedly only a few German painters gained international recognition during this time. One of them was Franz von Stuck, who was a founder member of *Secession* in Europe. Von Stuck had already achieved a social position, as he belonged to the 'Painter-Princes', the last of whom was Lenbach. Brought up in poor circumstances the talented von Stuck succeeded in only a few years in rising to the position of a professor in a recognised academy. While his technical ability came from the tradition of Lenbach, he stood, in terms of his themes, wholly under the heading of symbolism, alongside Fernand Khnopff. He also extended the use of certain elements to be found in the works of Arnold Bocklin.

As opposed to the erotic feminine figures of Moreau, who wore a cloak of secret rapture, of a dangerous dream, Franz von Stuck's women were emphatic and direct; even if exotically seductive. He painted the femme fatale.

The most important Art Nouveau painter in Berlin was Ludwig von Hofmann, who discovered Art Nouveau when studying French painters when he was a scholar at the Académie Julian in Paris. It was he who brought Gauguin's perceptions to Germany. It was also in Berlin that Art Nouveau found entry into the experiments of the artistic community via the Swiss, Cuno Amiet and the Finn, Axel Gallén, but only for a short but fruitful phase. Most notably, Karl Schmidt-Rottluff combined in some of his works elements of Art Nouveau with his otherwise rather dry conceptions.

The Munich artists on the editorial staff of the *Blauen Reiter* (Blue Knight) were also influenced by Art Nouveau. Paul Klee was a pupil of von Stuck. Franz Marc and Wassily Kandinsky produced a few pure Art Nouveau works. Here too, the style was primarily a means of freeing form and movement.

One circle of artists, the Worpswede Artists Union, who chose as their inspiration and workplace the sparsely impressive landscapes of the Devil's Moor in Worpswede near Bremen, came into the narrow circle of the Art Nouveau artists chiefly through one of its own members. While, amongst the founders of the artists' colony, Fritz Mackensen, Otto Modersohn, Hans am Ende and Paula Modersohn-Becker were only to be seen on the periphery of Art Nouveau, Heinrich Vogeler, who was, at least in 1892, a member of the group, was one of the most important masters of the new style in Germany. He was a friend of Rainer Maria Rilke, who once wrote about his paintings: 'The art of putting the whole of spring, the fulness and profusion of day and night into one flower, one branch, one birch tree, one homesick girl — this art is known to no-one as to Heinrich Vogeler'. Vogeler was, as opposed to his colleagues in the Worpswede Artists Union, no landscape painter. He was the spiritual cousin of the Englishmen: he valued Walter Crane highly and studied the writings of William Morris. Earlier, he had been invited to work on the English journal *The Studio*. Then *Insel* followed, for which he often produced the title page. Many more contracts for graphic collaboration followed. His designs graced the covers of numerous publications of note. His real mastery lay in the field of painting. Since his paintings have still not found any great entry into public collections, the importance of his works is under-estimated.

The works of the two artists Ferdinand Hodler and Giovanni Segantini hold a special position in Art Nouveau painting. Common to both of them is the unusual colour effect of their painting, from which one can deduce their origins in the clear mountain air of Switzerland. Hodler, in his choice and symbolic treatment of themes, which were enriched in the course of his life with expressionistic elements, exerted great influence on his colleagues in France and Germany.

Segantini was born in Italy but spent most of his life in Switzerland. He came from difficult circumstances, and arrived, only after some diversions, including impressionism, to a symbolistic painting of great clarity. The painters of Viennese Art Nouveau, the Secession group, showed themselves particularly open to his works. Segantini exhibited many times in Vienna, but also in London and Germany.

Although there were numerous artists living in Vienna and working in the Art Nouveau style, one particularly rose in their midst: Gustav Klimt. He began his painting career as a student of Hans Makart whose painting at the art-historical museum he studied in his early years. As a founder member of *Secession*, he was also their President. He was also one of the leading workers on *Ver Sacrum*, several issues of which were devoted to his works.

Klimt had a preference for murals. When he took the commission to decorate the main hall of Vienna University, he created, between 1900-1903, the painting-cycle, 'Philosophy, Medicine and Law', which with its permissive features unleashed a scandal on Vienna. Klimt brought to the stylised ornamentation of his allegorical figures a great sensuality and eroticism, which exposed him to attack.

Different influences, amongst them a visit to the mosaics of Ravenna, caused Klimt not only to ornament the background of his pictures – a process which at times even deformed the figures – but increasingly to replace this ornamentation with gold or silver leaf, which gave his works a pure Byzantine character. Evil tongues pointed out that Vienna lay closer to Byzantium than to Paris. He thus created harsh, closely-grouped naturalistic figures surrounded by fine geometric ornamentation.

The high point of Klimt's creativity arose from a building commission from the Belgian industrialist and art collector Adolphe Stoclet. He had lived in Vienna for a long time and found in the Viennese architect Josef Hoffmann the man who could realise his imaginings. Stoclet commissioned Hoffmann and the Viennese Workshops connected with him, to design and execute his palace. The murals were entrusted to Gustav Klimt. It was the greatest and most important work of his whole life. With this commission, the desire of Art Nouveau for the creation of a complete work of art became a reality. A whole house could be created throughout, with no financial limitations. So Brussels got, in the shape of the Palais Stoclet, a building which from the design stage to the furnishing was produced harmoniously in the spirit of Art Nouveau.

Arts and Crafts

The famous entrances to the Paris underground, the work of the French architect Hector Guimard, have already been referred to as especially striking examples of an artistic assignment with wide influence. It is less known that Guimard was also a sculptor and a cabinet maker. His Metro entrances are consequently a successful symbiosis of construction with applied sculpture and decoration. At the same time the demands of the Art Nouveau artists were fulfilled: that their creative work had to serve mankind, the general public.

A reform should bring together many things: consciousness of craftsmen's skills and faithfulness to materials which in a harmonically formed environment should change from materialism to the spirit. That implied a genuine reform of life, seen however from the point of view of the artists and craftsmen.

William Morris and his confederates tackled these thoughts of a new art both in theory and practice with considerable success. In France too, as our previous example shows, important contracts came quickly. In Germany it was at first a small circle of citizens from the upper classes who interested themselves in the new ideas and in the privacy of their own homes gave artists the chance to display their talents in terms of decoration and furnishing. From this circle were then recruited patrons with tasks for artists who served the general public. This not very large circle saw itself in the role of a taste-forming élite. Of particular note were Count Harry Graf Kessler and Grand Duke Ludwig von Hessen, whose artist colony of Mathildenhohe was a unique social project with far reaching effects. Then there was the Berlin circle around Walter Rathenau who knew how to motivate all the intelligent high financiers.

In the Western part of Germany it was the banker Karl Ernst Osthaus who not only founded the Folkwang Museum with his art school in Hessen, but also gave Henry von de Velde every encouragement and opportunity for display as his mentor.

In France only a few contributions to the history of art are not connected with Paris. In the arts and crafts of Art Nouveau it was the glassworks at Nancy in Lorraine, which was a leading producer of glasses and produced for that city an exceedingly honourable place alongside the capital. There was the Vererie Daum, a glass manufacturer which still exists today. But above all there was Emile Gallé, who provoked the international demand for glasses from Nancy. He was a universal genius. It was not just the magical glasses which he designed. He also understood how to integrate his outstanding artistic imagination in the industrial processes of a glass foundry, so that his works of art could be created in series. Moreover he ran – highly successfully – a great and economically important business. Not content with that, he also created Art Nouveau furniture, the design of which was innovative, and which he mass produced in a specially built factory, His greatest wish was to train new blood, adequately and according to the demands of high quality, to enable and ensure that his ideas had the greatest influence.

Apart from Gallé, Louis Majorelle, a friend of his who was a cabinet maker, produced items of furniture in his own factory, He divorced himself from the rather lavish designs of his friend by paying close attention to the organic structure that was inherent in a piece of furniture. Thus it is that today his furniture fulfils the demand for design that remains faithful to use and materials much more than that of Gallé.

Following an old tradition in France Art Nouveau furniture was always produced singly. i.e. every piece could and should stand on its own, show its own purpose and invite use. To show a complete furnished room was of less importance: the beauty of the individual piece was enough. Henry van de Velde was the first to work on the demand for the inclusive furnishing of whole rooms or dwellings. In Germany, where he immediately moved, van de Velde agreed completely with the concept which the young artists in Munich had when they planned the whole furnishing and equipment of rooms. They saw the design of the furniture as a detail of the internal architecture. These young architects were Richard Riemerschmid, Peter Behrens, Bernhard Pankok, August Endell and Bruno Paul. Above all, it was Pankok who succeeded in creating homogenously formed rooms with furniture that matched.

An opportunity for the buyer was provided in 1898 in Munich when the United Workshops for Arts and Crafts were founded. In Dresden the German Workshops arose almost simultaneously. These were associations of art and craft businesses which under the oversight and counsel of the designing artists guaranteed orderly production and organised distribution. The work of William Morris found late approval here.

What sort of effect Art Nouveau could have on the public becomes clear in the example of the artist, Hermann Obrist. He trained as a scientist and then went into arts and crafts. He created a number of embroideries in pure Art Nouveau form which were exhibited in 1894 in Munich. The general public took to this novelty with enthusiasm.

Jewellery was an area in which the grace and simplicity of Art Nouveau was particularly important. The jeweller René Lalique was closely connected with symbolism. His style has an effect like poetry transplanted to the smithy. The effect of his creations on his contemporaries, in comparison to the showy designs of the previous period must have been electrifying. He especially knew how to give his variegated art additional contrast with exquisite enamel and metallic inlaying and by using colourful semi-precious stones. Next to him there was chiefly Alphonse Maria Mucha and Eugène Grasset who were successful as jewellery designers. Taken together the French jewellers of this time represented supreme artistry.

A wealthy American business came forward as an important buyer of Parisian jewellery, the firm of Tiffany in New York, a giant concern specialising in jewellery, clocks and craft works. The first major contacts between the American house and France were the buying of Marie Antoinette's jewels in 1850, and in 1887 the buying of the French Crown Jewels (for which France has still not quite forgiven the USA even today). Louis Comfort Tiffany was the heir to this concern and kept it going successfully, even managing to become an artist himself. His interest was entirely for glass, to which he devoted his complete attention, admittedly without giving up the conscientious leadership of the empire he had inherited from his father. His personal style was always present in the work, although it came under the banner of Tiffany and Company Associated Artists. Not only was his glass manufacture great and technically brilliant, but also his design department consisted of an army of specialists.

In 1903 in Vienna Josef Hoffmann and Koloman Moser, with financial support from Fritz Warndorfer, decided to set up the Viennese Workshops Production Society of Craftworkers in Austria. Its main goal was the building and furnishing of houses, but it was also concerned with jewellery, metalwork, bookbinding and furniture. More artists soon joined the founder-members, almost all of them seceding from the Viennese Secession which lost importance in proportion to the rise of the Vienna Workshops. They set themselves a lofty task in their work programme and also acted in a manner consistent with the spirit of it.

In conclusion we will quote an extract:

"The boundless disaster which bad mass-production on the one hand, and the thoughtless imitation of the old style on the other, have produced in the area of arts and crafts, has flooded the world like a mighty river. To swim against the current is madness. Nevertheless we have set up our workshops. They will create for us, on home-ground, a still point amid the cheerful noises of trade. Those who know their debt to Ruskin and Morris will be welcome there. We call upon all those to whom culture seems worthwhile and hope that even the unavoidable mistakes of our friends will not stop us from promoting our cause."

129

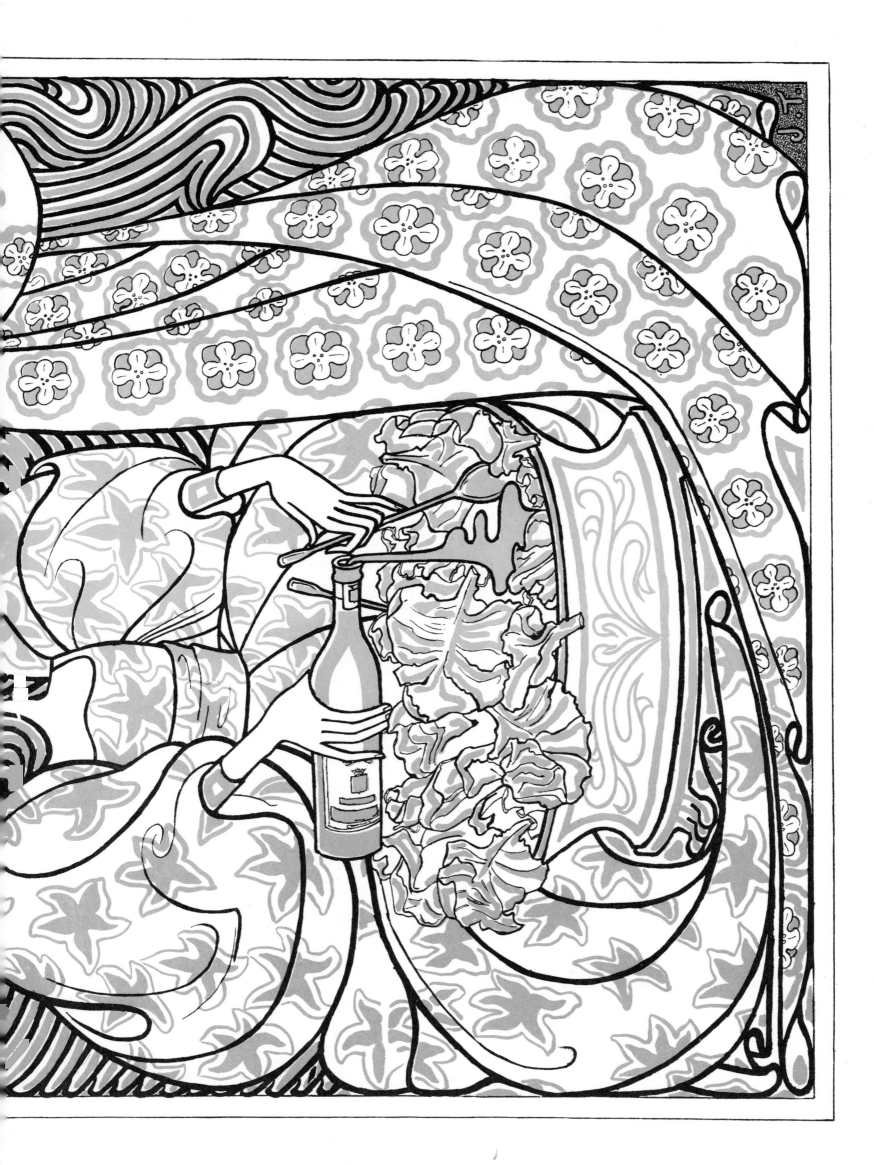

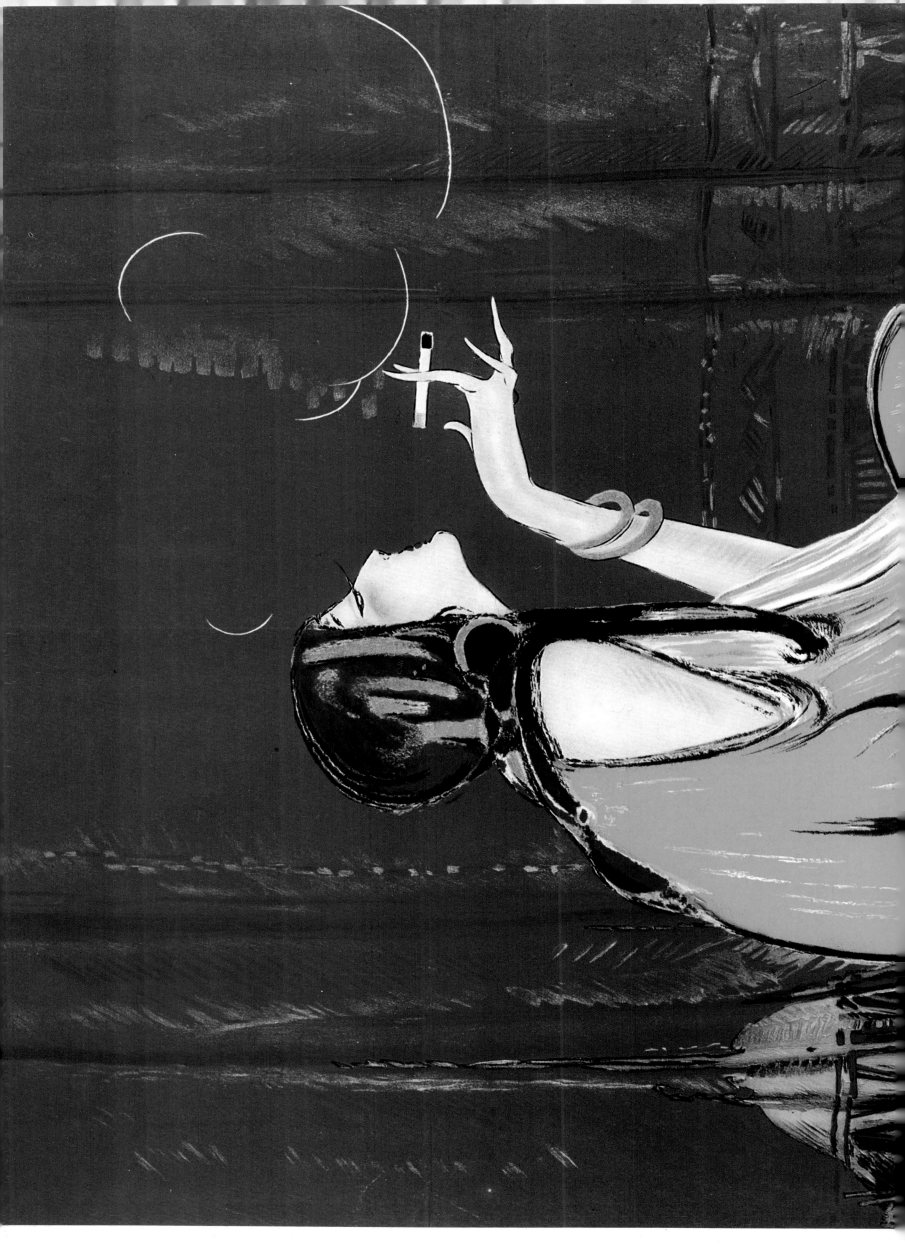

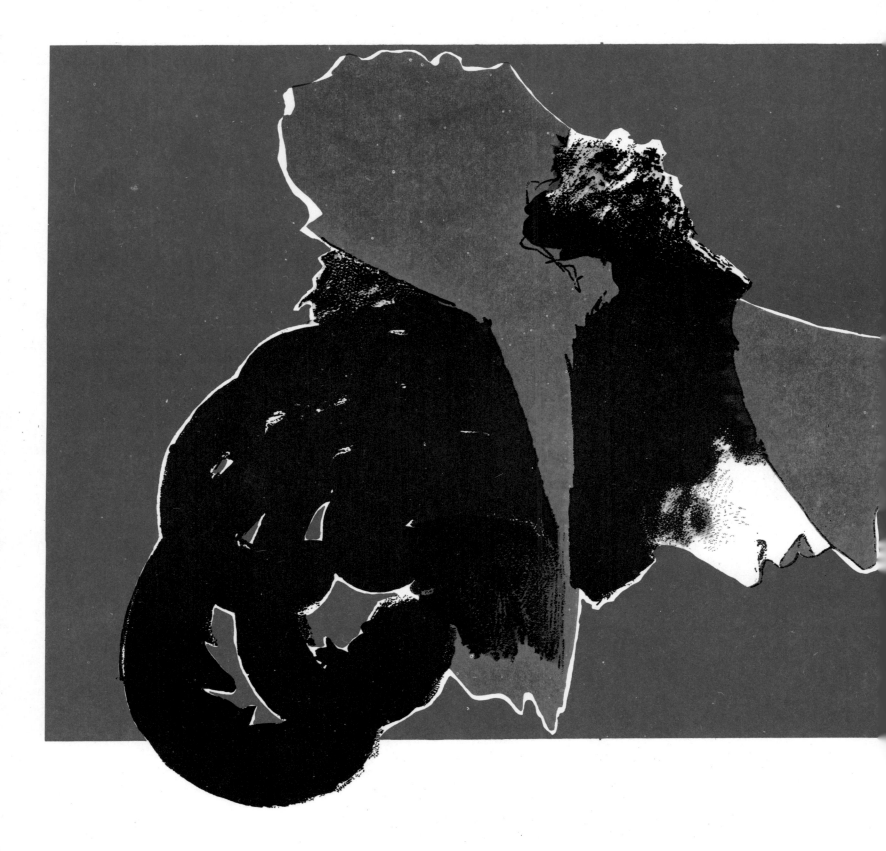

ESTAM-
PES &
ENCADRE-
MENTS
D'ART

Nº 1384

GRAVURES DU XVIIIᵐᵉ S.

NEDERLANDSCHE·VEREENIGING·DE·RIJWIEL·&·AUTOMOBIEL·INDUSTRIE

LOCK-TE MICH EIN IRR-LICHT HIN:

KOLO MOSER·

TABLE OF ILLUSTRATIONS